Modernists & *Mystics*

Edited by C. J. T. Talar

Modernists *& Mystics*

THE CATHOLIC UNIVERSITY
OF AMERICA PRESS

Washington, D.C.

The paper used in this publication meets the minimum requirements of American National Standards for Information Science—Permanence of Paper for Printed Library Materials, ANSI Z39.48-1984.
∞

Library of Congress Cataloging-in-Publication Data
Modernists and mystics / edited by C. J. T. Talar.
p. cm.
Includes bibliographical references and index.
ISBN 978-0-8132-1709-3 (cloth : alk. paper)
1. Modernism (Christian theology)—Catholic Church.
2. Mysticism—Catholic Church. I. Talar, C. J. T., 1947–
II. Title.
BX1396.M63 2009
248.2'20940903—dc22 2009010755

For Michael Kerlin (1936–2007), valued colleague, longtime contributor to the Roman Catholic Modernism Working Group/Seminar, and patient expositor of Blondel, who lightened our sessions with a touch of humor

Contents

Preface

William L. Portier

At the 1976 annual meeting of the American Academy of Religion (AAR), the late Ronald R. Burke of the University of Nebraska at Omaha convened the first session of a new consultation devoted to the study of what its members called Roman Catholic Modernism. The consultation soon graduated to become a permanent group. But after a review in 1994, the AAR program committee suppressed the group by refusing to renew its place on the program. It was given a five-year sunset reprieve until 1999. For twenty-three years, from 1976 up through 1999, the Roman Catholic Modernism Group (RCMG) continued to meet annually at the AAR.

Georgetown's Elizabeth McKeown has already made the RCMG the stuff of history. At a session of the Nineteenth-Century Theology Group at the 2001 annual meeting of the AAR in Denver, she thoroughly chronicled the Roman Catholic Modernism Group's twenty-three-year run. McKeown took the group's work as a case study in "how scholarship gets made—specifically in the fields of historical theology and the history of religion, and more generally in the major professional organization devoted to the study of religion in the United States."[1]

In the twenty-three preprinted copies of the group's working papers, one can track the state of the question on scholarship relating to

1. Elizabeth McKeown, "After the Fall: Roman Catholic Modernism at the American Academy of Religion," *U.S. Catholic Historian* 20/3 (Summer 2002): 111–31, at 113.

the Modernist crisis and the major figures involved in it. The longevity and continuity of the group, along with the practice of circulating papers and responses beforehand, contributed to a very high level of discussion.[2] In addition to many individual books and articles, the fruits of the group's near quarter century of collaboration include three topical, book-length collections: *Sanctity and Secularity during the Modernist Period: Six Perspectives on Hagiography around 1900* (Société des Bollandistes, 1999), edited by Lawrence Barmann and C. J. T. Talar; *Catholicism Contending with Modernity* (Cambridge University Press, 2000), edited by Darrell Jodock; and *Personal Faith and Institutional Commitments, Roman Catholic Modernist and Anti-Modernist Autobiography* (University of Scranton Press, 2002), edited by Lawrence Barmann and Harvey Hill.

All the contributors to the present volume belonged to the AAR's Roman Catholic Modernism Group. Lawrence Barmann and Michael Kerlin were charter members. C. J. T. Talar and Harvey Hill represent the group's second generation. *Modernists and Mystics* will be the fourth book-length contribution to come from the group.[3] The group's collaborative work over twenty-three years provides the deep context for each of the essays in the present volume.

Studying the Modernists Whole

This book is part of the authors' life after Modernism, in the AAR group sense. But the need for attention to life after Modernism for the Modernists was also a central insight of the group's work over the years. With the exception of George Tyrrell, the dramatis personae of the Modernist crisis lived well beyond the antimodernist encyclical *Pascendi dominici gregis* in 1907 and the imposition of the Oath against Mod-

2. Copies of the complete set of the Roman Catholic Modernism Group's working papers are preserved, thanks to Elizabeth McKeown, in the Roesch Library's U.S. Catholic Collection at the University of Dayton.

3. A book of biographies of those involved in the Modernist movement, Harvey Hill, Louis-Pierre Sardella, and C. J. T. Talar, *By Those Who Knew Them: French Modernists Left, Right, and Center* (Washington, D.C.: The Catholic University of America Press, 2008), also stems from the work done in the RCMG, although Saredella was not a member.

ernism in 1910. Of the subjects of this book's essays, von Hügel died in 1925, Albert Houtin a year later, Henri Bremond in 1933, Alfred Loisy in 1940, and Maurice Blondel in 1949. Given their subjects' longevity, an important part of the RCMG's work, therefore, was to contextualize in their lives as wholes the involvement in the crisis of the varied Modernist personae. This emphasis resulted in a turn to autobiographies written by Modernist figures and eventually in the book on the topic edited by Barmann and Hill.

The group's turn to autobiography is noteworthy for two reasons. First, it underscores the importance of what Barmann has called, with reference to Baron von Hügel, "the sense of his life's continuity, consistency, and slow development" derived by a scholar from "living in" the sources "patiently, repeatedly, thoroughly."[4] Each contributor has lived long in their subject's sources. Michael Kerlin, for example, could claim a study of Blondel "off and on for over forty years." Second, each chapter in this book develops Barmann's emphasis and contributes to the task of seeing their subjects, Friedrich von Hügel, Henri Bremond, Maurice Blondel, Albert Houtin, and Alfred Loisy, whole, in the long view of their life narratives.

In attempting to position the subjects of these essays with respect to modern mysticism, readers may find they are forced to position themselves. In this, a century later, we see the timeliness of the turn to the mystical by major figures involved in the Modernist crisis. By retrieving the Modernist figures' mystic turn, the contributors to *Modernists and Mystics* have demonstrated that, on the centenary of *Pascendi dominici gregis,* the lines that flow from the Modernist crisis continue to form the matrix of contemporary Catholic life.[5]

4. Lawrence Barmann, "Friedrich von Hügel as Modernist and as More than Modernist," *Catholic Historical Review* 75/2 (April 1989): 212.

5. In *Une Église en quête de liberté, La pensée catholique entre modernisme et Vatican II, 1914–1962* (Paris: Desclée de Brouwer, 1998), 10, Étienne Fouilloux argues that "the Modernist crisis is the intellectual matrix of contemporary Catholicism."

Modernists & *Mystics*

1 The Mystical Element of the Modernist Crisis

William L. Portier & C. J. T. Talar

Modernists and mystics make an incongruous combination. Or so it might appear. Urging an often-intransigent church into dialogue with modern science, critical history, historical critical studies of the Bible, and post-Kantian philosophy, those remembered as Modernists wanted to join the ancient faith to modern thought. We find the classic mystics, by contrast, in the past. In the West, we find them in late medieval and early modern Catholicism. But the figures associated with the Modernist crisis in Roman Catholicism not only looked forward in terms of critical history and philosophy. They also looked back into history to the church's mystical tradition. *Modernists and Mystics* tells the story of the Modernist turn to the mystical.

In a 1977 reassessment of the Modernist crisis, Nicholas Lash located it at the "beginning of a twentieth-century Catholic renaissance," an "in no small measure successful attempt to bring Catholicism 'up-to-date' with the world that came to birth between the seventeenth and nineteenth centuries."[1] Lash's reference to the seventeenth century re-

Portions of this chapter appeared originally as C. J. T. Talar, "The Historian and the Mystic: The Revisionist Vision of Henri Bremond," *Downside Review* 125 (2007): 177–96. Permission to reproduce this material here is gratefully acknowledged.

1. Nicholas Lash, "Modernism, Aggiornamento and the Night Battle," in *Bishops and Writ-*

calls the scientific revolution of that period and controversies over biblical criticism such as the one between Jacques-Bénigne Bossuet and Richard Simon. In the course of his article, however, Lash specifies the connection in what is perhaps a less expected way. He positions Wilfrid Ward, Friedrich von Hügel, and Maurice Blondel as looking, not to a "church of the future" but as finding their inspiration in models of the past. This is most obvious in the case of the Baron. But, as we shall see, it is also true of Henri Bremond, Maurice Blondel, and even Alfred Loisy.

> Von Hügel reached back, far beyond the polarities of the late nineteenth-century and found, in the "post-tridentine Church of the late seventeenth century," a forgotten tradition of wholeness, exemplified, above all, in such men as Fénelon and Mabillon. These men provided him with a "model" for that vision of reformed Catholicism for which he would work, and suffer, for the remainder of his life.[2]

Lash's reference to Fénelon requires a brief account of the Quietist controversy of the 1690s. For Fénelon and the controversy in which he found himself embroiled served not only the Baron, but also most of the other subjects of this book's essays, as paradigmatic for their own turns to the mystic.

Quietist Controversy as Paradigmatic

The grand century of Louis XIV was also the century of the Quietist controversies. In 1687 Pope Innocent XI censured sixty-eight propositions taken from the writings of Miguel de Molinos (1628–1696), a Spanish priest who advocated an exaggerated form of the prayer of quiet or acquired contemplation. Some of Molinos's disciples neglected vocal prayer and the sacraments and disregarded temptation in a way

---

ers, Aspects of the Evolution of Modern English Catholicism, ed. Adrian Hastings (Wheathampstead: Anthony Clarke, 1977), 51–79, at 76. We are grateful to William J. Collinge of Mount Saint Mary's University for his help with this chapter.

2. Ibid., 66, 67. Lash is quoting Thomas Loome, "The Enigma of Baron Friedrich von Hügel—as Modernist," *Downside Review* 91 (1973): 13–34; 123–40; 204–30. Lash expands Loome's insistence on the paradigmatic role of the Church of the seventeenth century for von Hügel to encompass also an earlier expression, the pre-Reformation Catholicism of the Renaissance.

that led to immorality. In France, Madame Jeanne Guyon's (1648–1717) *A Short and Easy Method of Prayer* (1685) taught a contemplative way that sought to quiet the emotions and the faculties and to rest in the presence of God. Many, including Jacques-Bénigne Bossuet (1627–1704), the formidable bishop of Meaux, interpreted Madame Guyon's teaching as leading, along the lines of the previously censured Quietism of Molinos, to disregard for the sacraments and traditional spiritual practices. Bossuet wrote to Madame Guyon. Her best-known advocate was a member of the royal court and later archbishop of Cambrai, François Fénelon (1651–1715). In response to Madame Guyon's own request, Bossuet assembled a conference at Issy outside Paris in 1695 to evaluate her spiritual doctrine. Despite Fénelon's defense of Madame Guyon and her teaching, the Articles of Issy (1695) censured thirty-four Quietist propositions having to do with the nature of pure or disinterested love and acquired contemplation. Though Madame Guyon signed the Articles of Issy, even Fénelon could not prevent her subsequent imprisonment, which lasted off and on until 1703. In *The Varieties of Religious Experience,* in his lecture on "Saintliness," William James used Madame Guyon's seeming indifference to her own imprisonment as an example of the active form "resignation" can take in "more optimistic" religious temperaments.[3]

Meanwhile, Fénelon went to Cambrai to take up the see to which he had been nominated before the assembly at Issy. From Cambrai in 1697, Fénelon published his *Explication des maximes des saints sur la vie intérieure* in which he invoked traditional spiritual writers to defend a notion of pure or disinterested love. Literary skirmishes with Bossuet followed. In 1699, Pope Innocent XII, seemingly under pressure from King Louis XIV and at the urgings of Bossuet, censured twenty-three propositions from *Explication des maximes des saints.* Fénelon immediately submitted.

At first glance, the Quietist controversies look like an obscure in-

3. William James, *The Varieties of Religious Experience, A Study in Human Nature, Being the Gifford Lectures on Natural Religion Delivered at Edinburgh in 1901–1902* (New York: New American Library, 1958), 227. On the Quietist controversies, we have followed the pertinent articles in *The Oxford Dictionary of the Christian Church,* 3rd ed. (New York: Oxford University Press, 1997).

tramural squabble among effete seventeenth-century French Catholics. But to the subjects of this book, the Quietist controversies were anything but obscure. Rather, they represent the beginning of a definitive narrowing and suffocating of Catholicism as a living religious tradition. This constriction and hyper-intellectualization of the tradition culminated in the established neoscholasticism of late nineteenth- and early twentieth-century manuals of theology. This view of the Quietist controversies as a decisive turning point in the tradition was shared especially by Bremond, Blondel, and even Loisy. In no one is this view of Quietism clearer than in the case of von Hügel. The name he gave to what began to be marginalized and lost in the seventeenth century was the "mystical element" of religion. His book on St. Catherine of Genoa is a full-scale attempt to re-credit the mystical element of the tradition in the face of the seventeenth-century censures of Quietism.

Von Hügel's Re-Crediting of the Mystical Element

In the figure of St. Catherine of Genoa (1447–1510), von Hügel's *The Mystical Element of Religion* returns to the time before the Reformation. But the Quietist controversies are never far from his mind. Abbé Henri Huvelin would have been instrumental in orienting von Hügel toward the seventeenth century and Fénelon in particular. With some regularity, the Baron recommends *Bossuet, Fénelon, le quiétisme* (1912), Huvelin's book on these figures.[4] In the middle of volume 2 of his great work, von Hügel includes a long section on Quietism. The height of the Quietist controversies was a time "when that mystical element must have seemed to many, to be discredited once for all." But the Baron goes on to say—in the same seven-line sentence—that even at such a time:

> Those best acquainted with the rich history of the Church, and with the manifold requirements of the abiding religious consciousness, could not and did not doubt that all that was good, deep, and true in that element would continue to be upheld and represented in the Church.[5]

4. On Huvelin, see Lucienne Portier, *Un précurseur: L'abbé Huvelin* (Paris: Cerf, 1979). From 1875 to 1884, Huvelin gave a series of lectures on the history of the church at Saint-Augustin in Paris. Fénelon and Quietism were covered in 1880.

5. Friedrich von Hügel, *The Mystical Element of Religion as Studied in Saint Catherine of*

In the face of this seemingly definitive discrediting, von Hügel appeals to the "rich history of the Church" to re-credit the mystical element.

Von Hügel bases his reading of the Quietist controversies on primary sources. And though he is careful to point out the errors in Quietism, which he located in its neglect of Christianity's incarnational center, he defends "Fénelon's moral and spiritual character, or deeply Catholic spirit and intentions" against Bossuet's "painfully fierce and unjust attack."[6] Likewise, von Hügel speaks up for Madame Guyon, "that much tried and vehemently opposed woman." He acknowledges the "largely misleading and indeed incorrect character of many of her analyses and expressions." But he goes on to point out that "many an undoubtedly Catholic-minded, experienced and close observer" held her to be "a truly saintly, entirely filial Catholic."[7]

With its doctrine of one act of faith that continues through life into eternity, the censured Quietism exaggerated what von Hügel identifies as the "specifically Neo-Platonist constituent" of older mystics. This led to the devaluing of the historical, institutional, bodily, and, in short, incarnational, aspects of Christianity. It is to older mystics in the wider tradition that von Hügel appeals to correct this exaggeration. But the "very eagerness with which it was welcomed at the time . . . as so much spiritual food and life by many a deeply religious soul" moved him to ask why Quietist doctrine was popular. What was its truth? He concludes that, despite its excess, what came to be known as Quietism was "divining and attempting to supply certain profound and abiding needs of the soul."[8]

He identified these needs as: (1) a human thirst for unity, for "a truly atomistic world . . . is utterly repulsive to any deeply religious spirit whose self-knowledge is at all equal to its aspirations"; (2) a need to purify oneself by detachment; (3) a need for admiration, trust, and faith, which leads to individual progress through absorption into something "clean and fruitful that can and does lift him out of and above his smaller self altogether;" and (4) a sense of shame in the spiritually awake at

Genoa and Her Friends, 2nd ed., 2 vols. (London: Dent, 1923), II: 142–43. Quietism is treated at length under the heading "Quietude and Passivity," 129–81.

6. Ibid., 140, 146, 141.

7. Ibid., 141.

8. Ibid., 148.

crediting virtue and spiritual insight to oneself. For each of these needs, quietists tended to choose between God and something other than God without realizing the "Incarnational action of God" as "the central truth and secret of Christianity."[9]

Von Hügel never drew explicit parallels between the Quietist controversies and the Modernist crisis. But these parallels were not lost on him. He described the "movement against the Quietists" as soon having "much of the character of a popular scare and panic." He found the "cruel injustice of many details and processes" of the campaign against Quietism "beyond dispute or justification."[10] Again, as he spoke of why Quietism drew so many deeply religious souls, he could not fail to note "the difficulty, and not infrequent ruthlessness of its suppression."[11] As he drew this long section on the Quietist controversies to a close, the Baron turned to the controversy over pure or disinterested love that had broken out between Fénelon and Bossuet after 1695. Again, he defended Fénelon in the strongest terms. As to his "pure and spiritual character and deeply Catholic intentions there has never been any serious doubt."[12] He gave his last word on this controversy to Fénelon:

> I know well that men misuse the doctrines of Pure Love and Resignation; I know that there are hypocrites who, under cover of such noble terms, overthrow the Gospel. Yet it is the worst of all procedures to attempt the destruction of perfect things, from a fear that men will make wrong use of them . . . the very perfection of Christianity is Pure Love.[13]

Blondel, Loisy, and Bremond on Fénelon

When Blondel and Loisy are discussed in relation to the Modernist crisis, attention naturally gravitates toward matters of critical exegesis and critical philosophy, rather than to spirituality in general or to the Quietist controversies in particular. The two imposing volumes of von Hügel's *Mystical Element of Religion*, and his own treatment of Quietism, make spirituality harder to ignore in his case. But this aspect of

9. Ibid., 148–50.
10. Ibid., 145.
11. Ibid., 148.
12. Ibid., 160.
13. Ibid., 181.

his work is often seen as idiosyncratic and separate from his Modernist involvement. It was not. Rather, as Lawrence Barmann has argued elsewhere and reiterates in this volume, von Hügel was a Roman Catholic Modernist precisely because he was a Roman Catholic mystic.

But there is good reason to think that Blondel and even Loisy also viewed the Quietist controversies as a crucial turning point and Fénelon as a model from whom they drew inspiration. Nicholas Lash places Blondel alongside von Hügel as one who searched for a model of reformed Catholicism by reaching back beyond nineteenth-century scholasticism to a time before the Quietist controversies, a time that represented a deeper and more whole Catholic history.

For Blondel, as for von Hügel, the "obscuring" of this tradition occurred decisively with the condemnation of Quietism. The Quietist controversy marked "the origin of the divorce between Catholicism and living thought, genuine art and scholarship which Blondel and his generation (who rediscovered the spiritual tradition) were the first to recognize, understand and reverse."[14]

Loisy, for his part, professed a militant sympathy for Quietism, since he identified *pur amour* as the very essence of Christianity, the religion closest to the religious ideal.[15] Bremond's *Apologie pour Fénelon* impressed Loisy; it was a book he read and reread. In his *George Tyrrell et Henri Bremond,* Loisy defended it in print, while rendering a negative judgment on the influence of Bossuet:

In crushing Richard Simon, Bossuet retarded the movement of biblical criticism in our country by almost two centuries and rendered such a movement nearly impossible in the Catholic Church; in getting mixed up with the reunion of Protestant communities with the Roman Church, he only succeeded in rendering this reunion impossible; in solemnly defaming Fénelon and Mme Guyon, he as much as killed high mysticism in France, and thus contributed greatly to the weakening of religion in our country.[16]

14. Lash, "Modernism," 71. Quoting Alexander Dru and Illtyd Trethowan, *Maurice Blondel: The Letter on Apologetics and History and Dogma* [1964] (Grand Rapids, Mich.: Eerdmans, 1994), 24.

15. See Raymond de Boyer de Saint-Suzanne, "Alfred Loisy et la religion du pur amour," *Commentaire* 3 (1978): 304–15.

16. Alfred Loisy, *George Tyrrell et Henri Bremond* (Paris: Émile Nourry, 1936), 88–89.

In 1917 Loisy published *La Religion,* an early statement of the kind of religious and moral philosophy that we find in the 1934 work that is the subject of Harvey Hill's essay in this volume. "I have given its place to mystical experience," he wrote in a letter to Maude Petre about the book and its reception. His notion of faith, he noted, "struck Bergson" but "will appear to scientists the height of mysticism." Loisy reserved his opinion about specific mystical doctrines, which he took to be "more or less special and relative as conditioned by time and environment." But then he added,

> I think the great mystics would be, in a certain way, the most indulgent critics of my essay, and I have already written to Bremond that our father Fénelon would not have cursed me. He would only have thought that I had perused the *Maximes des Saints* less than *Télémaque.*[17]

Télémaque was an educational novel that Fénelon wrote during the years he served at the royal court as tutor to King Louis XIV's grandson. As a work intended to instruct a future king, *Télémaque* emphasized the moral limits on royal power. Such implied criticism drew the ire of King Louis. In this comment, Loisy expressed both his real admiration for Fénelon as well as his characteristic reserve.

Maude Petre's last and posthumously published book, from which this letter is cited, is too much neglected. Her book's express purpose was to present Loisy not as a mere critic but as a serious religious figure. His later ideas on morality and mysticism, Petre argued, were closer to those of his early life than the works he produced during the later Modernist crisis and its aftermath. The idea of Loisy as Fénelon's spiritual descendant, and even as a mystic, was perfectly in keeping with her intent.

Charles Talar's essay in this volume demonstrates Fénelon's paradigmatic stature for Henri Bremond. It is telling that, after publishing three volumes of Newman texts for the series *La Pensée chrétienne* and a psychological biography on Newman, Bremond left Newman behind, as it were, and turned toward the seventeenth century.[18] His *Apologie*

17. Alfred Loisy to Maude Petre, Paris, September 29, 1917, as cited in Maude Petre, *Alfred Loisy, His Religious Significance* (Cambridge: Cambridge University Press, 1944), 83.

18. Henri Bremond, *Newman I. Le développement du dogme Chrétien* (Paris: Libraire

pour Fénelon was followed by the volumes of the monumental *Histoire littéraire du sentiment religieux en France.* As with von Hügel and Blondel, Bremond sought in that century resources for the church of his own day. The interest among all of these men, along with Loisy, in the spirituality of mysticism might appear surprising. It becomes less so, if account is taken of the renewed interest in mysticism present in both Catholic and secular circles in the later 1890s.

Context for the Modernist Turn to Mysticism

While the outcome of Bossuet's controversy with Fénelon was to discredit mysticism for the next two centuries within Roman Catholicism, mysticism did not disappear. Within the Church, however, mystics were left to their spiritual directors, and the study of their experiences to a restricted circle of specialist theologians. Outside Catholicism, mysticism tended to be identified with abnormality or assimilated to the occult. Toward the end of the nineteenth century, with the occurrence of a revival of interest in mystical phenomena, this state of affairs began to change. David Knowles attributed the new situation principally to two sources, stemming from different quarters and motivated by different reasons. The scientific study of psychology, "conducted primarily by nonbelievers or those unorthodox by traditional theological standards" utilizing empirical methods, focused on religious phenomena "only as providing further instances of unusual psychological conditions."[19]

Within Catholic circles, as a reaction against the prevailing rationalism—presumably the scientific positivism and materialism at work in the larger culture as well as the rationalist tenor of neoscholastic theology—attention was directed toward the personal experiences of contemporaries or those described in the writings of celebrated mys-

Bloud, 1905; 2nd ed., 1906); *Newman II. Psychologie de la foi* (Paris: Libraire Bloud, 1905); *Newman III. La vie Chrétienne* (Paris: Libraire Bloud, 1906); *Essai de biographie psychologique* (Paris: Bloud & Gay, 1906); *The Mystery of Newman,* trans. H. C. Corrance (London: Williams & Norgate, 1907).

19. David Knowles, "What Is Mysticism?" in *Understanding Mysticism,* ed. Richard Woods (Garden City, N.Y.: Image Books, 1980), 521–22. In addition to the new religious psychology, the study of comparative religion has also been identified as a factor (5).

tics of the past. Interestingly, despite the diversity of sources, there was something of a convergence of approach: "most of these Catholic thinkers, in this resembling the psychologists, approached the subject from outside, with a quasi-scientific technique of observing and comparing phenomena in hope of arriving at general conclusions and a definition of their subject."[20]

The Psychologists

Readers familiar with Émile Zola's trilogy *Les trois villes,* especially its first volume *Lourdes,* will already be acquainted with the theories of Jean-Martin Charcot (1825–1893). The period from 1870 to 1914 has been characterized as "the golden age of hysteria," during which the medical use of the term broadened into an aesthetic and then into a more general cultural category.[21] Charcot's work at the Salpêtrière and his popular writings played an important role in this process of diffusion.[22] In "La foi qui guérit" he attributed the success of many "miraculous cures" to the hysterical origins of the condition and its overcoming through external suggestion or autosuggestion. In short, faith healing could be explained naturalistically. While mysticism is not the focus of his interest in this article, it is clear that he regards it as likewise rooted in hysteria.[23] For Charcot and those, such as Albert Houtin, influenced by him, mysticism assumed the guise of a pathological face of nature, not that of saintly ecstasy.

Pierre Janet, who had worked in Charcot's neurology wards at the Salpêtrière, was one of those so influenced. Janet introduced a refine-

20. Ibid., 522.

21. Christina Mazzoni, *Saint Hysteria: Neurosis, Mysticism, and Gender in European Culture* (Ithaca: Cornell University Press, 1996), 2.

22. "So powerful was his influence in the 1880s that the Salpêtrière was often called the 'Hôpital Charcot,' and the group of disciples and admirers around him was known as the *charcoterie.*" Elaine Showalter, "Hysteria, Feminism, and Gender," in *Hysteria Beyond Freud,* Sander L. Gilman, et al. (Berkeley: University of California Press, 1993), 307. On Charcot, see Georges Guillain, *J.-M. Charcot, sa vie son oeuvre* (Paris: Masson, 1955).

23. J.-M. Charcot, "La foi qui guérit," *La Revue hebdomadaire* 7 (Dec. 1892): 112–32. St. Francis of Assisi and St. Teresa of Avila are identified as "undeniable hysterics" (117). Mazzoni remarks that "because of her prolonged illness and the sensuality permeating her writings," among Christian mystics St. Teresa "has traditionally been the 'privileged' target of the hysteria-mysticism interpretive tug-of-war" (*Saint Hysteria,* 37).

ment that was to prove pregnant with possibility: the idea of the secondary self. This was predicated upon a dissociative model of consciousness that "in effect, postulated that chains of bodily memories, if sufficiently extensive and elaborate, could in turn constitute distinct selves or personalities."[24] This provided a theoretical model for understanding how two "selves" could coexist in one body. Manifesting his indebtedness to Charcot, Janet viewed all displays of a secondary self as symptomatic of hysteria.[25] Others, by contrast, believed that such secondary centers of consciousness could reside in healthy subjects. Rather than see the divided mind with Janet as defective, and the healthy mind as unified, it was possible to think of the mind as naturally multiplex. When the theory of the secondary self was joined to the notion of the subconscious self, a basis was formed for understanding a whole range of religious phenomena, including mysticism, as potentially positive and healthy experiences while not denying the possibility of pathology.

In the United States, William James became a proponent of this approach and we shall return to him in the following. While James's work was influential in France, a native exponent of this recourse to the subconscious may be found in Henri Delacroix, whose *Études d'histoire et de psychologie du mysticisme* appeared in 1908. Posing the question, "does the pathological hypothesis explain the totality or at least the essential of mystical states, does it explain the law of their succession?" Delacroix deemed it "incontestable" that the hypothesis explained a great deal.[26] This was eminently the case with "mystics of an inferior order, whose feats an intrepid hagiography and a prodigiously ignorant literature of edification have collected."[27] With, however, the "great mystics," those representative of "the richest and most complete form of Catholic mysticism," something more was at work. Just as artistic genius cannot be

24. Ann Taves, *Fits, Trances, & Visions* (Princeton: Princeton University Press, 1999), 255.

25. See Elisabeth Bronfen, *The Knotted Subject: Hysteria and Its Discontents* (Princeton: Princeton University Press, 1998), 279–89, for elaboration of Janet's views.

26. Writing in 1911, Jules Pacheu noted Delacroix as "at present . . . one of the most prominent, and most authoritative exemplars of purely naturalist theorists." Jules Pacheu, *L'Expérience mystique et l'activité subconsciente* (Paris: Perrin, 1911), 71.

27. Henri Delacroix, *Études d'histoire et de psychologie du mysticisme* (Paris: Félix Alcan, 1908), 341.

reduced to pathological states, neither may religious genius be fully accounted for in those terms.[28] "Hysteria in and of itself does not explain Saint Teresa, any more than mental derangement, or neurosis explains the long series of geniuses and talented people who have manifested its symptoms."[29] While an apparent mysticism can be explained pathologically, in forms typical of the great mystics there exists intuition and insight distinguishable from accompanying organic and psychological disorders.

The dissociative model of consciousness rendered possible a naturalistic explanation of mystical intuition on these terms. Janet had maintained that the subconscious could assume an autonomous life and development in complete independence from the conscious mental state. Thus a secondary self could exist without the subject's awareness of this division in mental states found in the hysterical personality. This independence of subconscious and conscious states reappears in Delacroix's more positive evaluation of mysticism. Such experiences have their origin in subconscious activity, in spontaneous, creative, and fundamentally indeterminate intuitions that, in the process of coming to conscious expression and possession, are always already shaped by determinate traditions.

Access to the subconscious can be cultivated; hence the role played by ascetical practice in the lives of mystics. The products of subconscious activity are presented to consciousness, which does not recognize them as its work. Instead, guided by tradition, the subject interprets them as the operation of divine action within the self. Thus "mystical experience, such as mystics represent it, is less a raw experience, a pure datum, than an experience already systematized, interpreted, penetrated by doctrine."[30] And hence Delacroix's conviction that "the most sublime states of mysticism in no way exceed the power of

28. Ibid., ii, vii.

29. Ibid., 342.

30. Ibid., 348. Maurice Blondel faulted Delacroix for focusing exclusively on the interpretive role played by religious traditions on "the facts" while being insufficiently attentive to that played by the psychological tradition. See Augustin Poulain, *Des Grâces d'oraison* (Paris: Gabriel Beauchesne, 1931), 615–16. *The Graces of Interior Prayer,* English trans. Leonora L. Yorke Smith (St. Louis: B. Herder, 1951), 580–81.

nature; religious genius suffices to explain its grandeur as sickness its weaknesses."[31] Subconscious states are not necessarily inferior states. The subconscious is not necessarily productive of aberration; it is also the principle of humanity's accomplishments. Delacroix gained the respect of Catholics—though not their agreement—for his sympathetic treatment of the mystics he studied, the value of those studies, and his evident sincerity.[32]

Catholic Sources

Turning to Catholic sources of a revival of interest in mysticism, it is noteworthy that signs of such interest were not much in evidence even toward the end of the 1890s. In October 1898 George Tyrrell wrote to Bremond,

> I am completely in agreement with you with regard to the coldness of modern Catholic piety as compared to a certain mystical current among Protestants; but I imagine that it concerns a relatively recent trait in both; a reaction of the latter against the aridity of the rationalist spirit which is the soul of Protestantism, while Catholics, in opposition to the "fluency of the word," to the indeterminate character, the sentimentalism of Protestants, have insisted on definitions and reason to an extreme that has killed mysticism for the time being.[33]

This state of affairs was soon to change, at least on the Catholic side. In early 1901, the Jesuit Augustin Poulain published *Des Grâces d'oraison Traité de théologie mystique.* Augmented over the next several years and running through many editions (by 1914 it had reached its ninth and been translated into four languages), it can be said to have "popularized mysticism." Poulain "opened, or rather reopened, a road almost closed to the great majority since the seventeenth century."[34]

31. Delacroix, *Études,* xix.

32. Pacheu, *L'Expérience,* 71 and n. 71.

33. Letter dated 29 October 1898 in Ann Louis-David, *Lettres de George Tyrrell à Henri Bremond.* (Paris: Aubier Montaigne, 1971), 43. Note: Louis-David translated Tyrrell's letters into French. Lacking access to the originals, I have rendered her French back into English. The quoted text therefore represents Tyrrell's ipsissima vox rather than his ipsissima verba.

34. Poulain, *Grâces,* xlvi, and *Graces,* lxvii, in J. V. Bainvel's introduction. Despite its subtitle Poulain wanted to fashion a study that was descriptive, rather than theoretical or doctrinal.

Two years after the appearance of Poulain's book, Auguste Saudreau's *L'État mystique* came out. When Saudreau published *Les Faits extraordinaires de la Vie spirituelle* in 1908 as the "sequel" and "complement" to his earlier study, he remarked, "over the past several years mystical studies had gained in reputation."[35] These were the two names that achieved prominence in Catholic circles in the years preceding Bremond's work. They of course did not stand alone. But they came to be seen as the representatives of two distinguishable tendencies in approaching mysticism.[36] Some of the issues that differentiate them relate to rather technical points in mystical theology and need not detain us here.

In light of Bremond's *Histoire,* however, two issues may be highlighted. The first concerns the prevalence of mystical graces. Against a school of thought which considered contemplative graces as supplementary, accessory, and thus given infrequently (of which Poulain was a recent exponent), Saudreau held them to be "the normal term of the spiritual life."[37] Second and closely related to the question of the incidence of mystical experience, is another concerning its fundamental nature. According to Poulain, in the mystic state God gives "an experimental, intellectual knowledge" of his presence, "analogous to that of the senses which do not reason." In ordinary prayer, "the soul *thinks* of God" whereas in mystic union "it *really feels* Him." The former results from a human act of will; the second occurs only upon God's initiative. The "abyss" separating "ordinary prayer from the mystic union" thus differentiates ascetic from mystical states and is consonant with the conviction that the latter tend to be exceptional.[38]

Saudreau demurs. He counters that "this sentiment of the presence

See Émile Goichot, *Henri Bremond. Historien du sentiment religieux* (Paris: Éditions Ophrys, 1982), 95.

35. Auguste Saudreau, *Les Faits extraordinaires de la Vie spirituelle* (Paris: Vic & Amat, 1908), 5, 9.

36. Writing on the "Present State of Mystical Studies" in 1921, Bainvel saw Poulain and Saudreau as influential representatives of what he termed the "Teresian Group" and the "Ascetico-mystical Group," respectively. A revised form of this survey appears in Bainvel's introduction to Poulain, *Grâces,* xlvi–lxvi and *Graces,* lxvii–lxxxvi.

37. Auguste Saudreau, *L'État mystique* (Paris: Vic & Amat, 1903), 18–20; *Mystical State,* vii–viii. Cf. *Faits extraordinaires,* 169–72.

38. Poulain, *Grâces,* 69–73; *Graces,* 64–67. Cf. Saudreau, *État mystique,* 127; *Mystical State,* 76.

of God in the soul" is not essential to the mystical experience, but constitutes only one of its varieties. Its constituent elements are twofold: "a superior knowledge of God, which, although general and confused, gives a very high idea of his incomprehensible greatness," and "an unreasoning but very precious love which God himself communicates, and to which the soul, in spite of all its efforts, could never raise itself."[39]

To tensions affecting French Catholicism in the wake of the condemnations of Modernism were added those stemming from differences between these two schools of mystical interpretation. They confronted each other with increasing asperity.

Modernists as Mystics

The chapters in this book deal successively with the mystic turn as found in Friedrich von Hügel, Henri Bremond, Maurice Blondel, Albert Houtin, and Alfred Loisy. From the time of his 1972 book on Baron Friedrich von Hügel, Lawrence Barmann has insisted on the need, as he put it in 1989, "to study von Hügel whole," to see him "in a larger context than that of the Modernist crisis "in order to see him more accurately within the Modernist context."[40] Barmann has done this most thoroughly in his chapter on "The Modernist as mystic" in *Catholicism Contending with Modernity.* Barmann's contribution to this volume is a coda to "The Modernist as Mystic." In this present chapter, Barmann uses the Baron's 1904 essay on "Official Authority and Living Religion" to illumine the claim that von Hügel was a Modernist precisely because he was a mystic. Barmann's use of the term "mystic" aims to identify the Baron's life-long project of religious integration.

As we have seen, the seventeenth-century Quietist controversy is paradigmatic for the mystic turn taken by many involved in the Modernist crisis. Of no one is this truer than of Henri Bremond. Charles Talar's chapter on Bremond follows the latter's retrieval of François Fénelon from the 1910 "nodal point in Bremond's personal journey" up through

39. Saudreau, *État mystique,* 111–12; *Mystical State,* 77, 65.

40. Lawrence Barmann, "Friedrich von Hügel as Modernist and as More Than Modernist," *Catholic Historical Review* 75/2 (April 1989): 211.

his later works, including the great eleven-volume *Histoire littéraire du sentiment religieux,* throughout which Talar detects the presence of Fénelon. Indeed, Talar argues, Bremond saw in Fénelon's situation and his loyalty to Madame Guyon certain similarities with his own situation and loyalty to George Tyrrell as he lay dying. It was Bremond who gave Tyrrell the last rites. Bremond suffered censure for that and for praying at Tyrrell's graveside in the Anglican cemetery at Storrington. In Talar's hands, Bremond's later historical work on Fénelon becomes part of our understanding of what Bremond was doing in 1909 at the height of the Modernist crisis.

Michael Kerlin's chapter on Blondel begins with Blondel's 1925 essay, "Le problème de la mystique." Kerlin ranges over Blondel's works "from his first days as a student of philosophy to his final writings." He argues that for Blondel philosophy finds its consummation in *la mystique* (the mystical) as an integrative union of knowledge, action, and being in a form of prayer. In *la mystique* philosophy reaches the "sanctity of reason," seeing, in Blondel's words, "through the eyes of the Mediator." Philosophers re-enact the very act of charity from which they have their being. Rather than manifesting itself in some extraordinary phenomenon, Blondel's *la vraie et seule mystique* rests in a certain contemplative sense of what the philosopher is doing all the time.

Of all the characters in the Modernist drama, Albert Houtin is probably the least sympathetic. *Bitter* and *negative* are the two words most frequently used to describe him. Upon reading the draft of Houtin's *Histoire du modernisme catholique* (1913), von Hügel lamented to Maude Petre "the writer's all pervading corrosive embitterment."[41] In 1925, the year before his death, Houtin published *Une grande mystique, Madame Bruyère.* Despite its title, the book is largely an exposé of Mère Cécile Bruyère (1845–1909), abbess of the women's abbey at Solemnes. Houtin includes a memorandum to the Holy Office, written in 1891 by a monk with psychoanalytic training who had been under Mère Cécile's spiritual direction. *Une grande mystique* allows Houtin to return to an episode

41. Von Hügel to Petre, October 15, 1912, as cited by Barmann in "The Modernist as Mystic," in *Catholicism Contending with Modernity,* 245, n. 68.

early in his life when he had been a novice at Solemnes in 1887. Houtin's *Une grande mystique,* as Talar's analysis shows, grants us access both to Houtin's own "radically positivist epistemology of religious experience" and to a clinical perspective contemporary with the Modernist crisis, that of Jean-Martin Charcot and his category of "moral hysteria."

Harvey Hill's treatment of Loisy's 1934 critique of Henri Bergson's *Two Sources* is a chapter in Hill's broader engagement with Loisy's life as a whole. This effort is best seen in Hill's contribution to *Personal Faith and Institutional Commitments* where he uses Loisy's various autobiographies to show him as "more than a biblical critic." This, as we have seen, was also the point of Maude Petre's 1944 book on Loisy's religious significance. In tacking back to 1902 in the last section of his present chapter, Hill sheds light on Loisy's purposes in *L'Évangile et l'Église.* Against Bergson, Loisy invokes the category of mysticism as the single source of religion and morality. Loisy understood mysticism very broadly as the social solidarity that Bergson limited to static religion and closed morality. To the extent that all four of our authors attempt to see their subject whole, they follow the path laid out by Barmann in his pioneering work on von Hügel.

From *Mystique* to *La Mystique*

Until the late medieval period, in both Greek and Latin Christian usage, the adjective "mystical" tended, with some variation, of course, to be used to describe various embodied activities, Christian practices such as reading the Scriptures and praying either liturgically or in personal devotion.[42] Focusing on the sixteenth and seventeenth centuries, Michel de Certeau's *Mystic Fable* traces a process by which the adjective *mystique* became the substantive *la mystique.* The noun form portrayed the quarantine of the interior from embodied forms of Christian reading and praying, the separation of piety from theology. (Recall von Hügel's critique of Quietism as anti-incarnational.) The adjective

42. See Louis Dupré, "Mysticism," in *The Encyclopedia of Religion,*" ed. Mircea Eliade (New York: Macmillan, 1987), 10: 245–61, at 245–46.

that had been used to modify "theology" became a separate noun that demarcated a new area or field of knowledge with its own discourse. What had once been particular experiences became the principles that governed this new discourse, that is, the language of the purgative, illuminative, and unitive ways.[43]

Building on this work, Leigh Schmidt has traced Certeau's new mystic tradition from seventeenth-century France to England, where John Wesley read Fénelon and the language of the Quietist controversies became a staple of enlightened polemic against Methodists and Quakers. Eventually, in the decades before the subjects of this book began to write, the English noun "mysticism" emerged and appeared in the *Encyclopedia Britannica* in 1858. Schmidt traces its path through American Transcendentalism earlier in the nineteenth century, to its flowering with William James at the beginning of the twentieth century into what Schmidt calls "Modern mysticism." Now, in the early twenty-first century, according to Schmidt, it is "a category in disrepair, sunk in the disrepute of its multiple occlusions."[44]

In bringing this introductory chapter to a close, it is worthwhile to ask how the subjects of each subsequent chapter might be positioned with respect to the evolution from *mystique* to *la mystique*, from the mystical of Christian tradition to Schmidt's essentialized modern mysticism. Given Schmidt's analysis, how useful is mysticism? In the hands

43. Michel de Certeau, *The Mystic Fable*, vol. 1, *The Sixteenth and Seventeenth Centuries*, trans. Michael B. Smith (Chicago: University of Chicago Press, 1992), 16, 76–77, 107–13. The original French edition appeared in 1982. Certeau builds on the work of Henri de Lubac, with whom he studied briefly in the period before Lubac's teaching career was cut short in 1950 in the controversy surrounding *la nouvelle théologie* and the encyclical *Humani Generis.* As he takes up the question of the evolution of the term *mystique* at the end of the Middle Ages, Certeau invokes Lubac's *Corpus Mysticum* to which he understands *Mystic Fable* as a possible sequel. The term *corpus mysticum,* he writes, "has the advantage of having been the object of a detailed theological study to which my history might be the sequel," at 79, and 315, n. 10, where Certeau cites the second edition of *Corpus Mysticum* (1949). Lubac and Certeau did not always see eye to eye. See the treatment of their relationship in Natalie Zemon Davis, "The Quest of Michel de Certeau," *New York Review of Books* 55/8 (May 15, 2008). See also Louis Dupré's comments on the "pre-existing niches of purification, illumination, and union" as exemplifying the new mystic discourse described by Certeau in *The Enlightenment and the Intellectual Foundations of Modern Culture* (New Haven: Yale University Press, 2004), 318.

44. Leigh Eric Schmidt, "The Making of Modern 'Mysticism,'" *Journal of the American Academy of Religion* 71/2 (June 2003): 273–302, at 274.

of the Modernists and their interpreters, is it more than the empty abstraction Schmidt describes?

The terms "mystical" or "mysticism" appear in each contribution to this volume. As Hill remarks, Loisy, in his critique of Bergson, had already raised the danger of essentializing the term. In fact, the position Hill describes as Loisy's in 1934 would be congenial to many contemporaries in religious studies. Barmann and Talar use mystic and mysticism in the very specifically located cases of von Hügel and Bremond and their historical studies of Catherine of Genoa and Archbishop François Fénelon of Cambrai. Von Hügel sought in the Genoese saint a representative of a very specific tradition he wanted to retrieve, described by Barmann as large-souled, pre-Protestant, pre-Tridentine Catholicism also represented by Nicholas of Cusa. Among post-Tridentine Catholics, it was Fénelon, von Hügel thought, who came closest to this ideal.[45]

The Modernists tended to see their own conflicts with the Vatican reflected in Fénelon's struggle with Bossuet. As Talar shows, Bremond saw his own support of Tyrrell reflected in Fénelon's support of Madame Guyon. In the overdetermined ecclesiastical atmosphere of the Modernist crisis, those who contended with latter day Bossuets tried to retrieve Fénelon's apophatic contemplative ideal as a type of their own way of immanence. Were they doing more than so-called modern mysticism?

In terms of Certeau's description of the evolution from *mystique* to *la mystique,* the integrative efforts of von Hügel and Blondel can best be read as returning to mystical as a modifier pointing to a dimension of theology, prayer, and life. This is clearest in von Hügel, especially in his sympathetic critique of Quietism as anti-incarnational. It is also clear in Kerlin's account of Blondel. Both von Hügel and Blondel tried to liberate from isolation and reconnect what the Baron referred to as the "elements" of an organic and whole religious life. In von Hügel's terms, Certeau describes these elements as having been quarantined from one another, around the time of the Quietist controversies, with the mystical element confined to a new mystic tradition. Von Hügel wanted to

45. Barmann, "Friedrich von Hügel," 217–18.

set the mystical element free from its interior confinement to regather and to revivify the other elements.

Responding to critics in the 1923 preface to the second edition of *The Mystical Element of Religion,* von Hügel tried to describe something like the immanence of God's transcendence.[46] He was concerned not so much with "any awareness or experience which could properly be called mystical, and which we could nevertheless hold to be universally prevalent." Rather, he was concerned with "the question as to the implications of all our knowledge . . . and as to whether we do not all, as a matter of fact, act and think in ways fully explicable only as occasioned and determined, in some of their most striking features, by the actual influence of the actually present God."[47]

As Kerlin explains, Blondel, like Certeau after him, rejects the noun *mysticisme* in favor of *la mystique.* When he wrote "Le problème de la mystique" in 1925, the term *mysticisme* carried connotations Blondel wanted to distinguish from his Christian-specific notion of *la vraie et seule mystique.* In strong language Blondel dismisses the moods and sentiments associated with the term "mysticism" as "smoky ardors of instinct, troubled effusions of sentiment, cloudy sublimities of passion, bad and good romanticism, the ecstasies of the flesh and ravishments of the spirit." The wise, Blondel concludes, are rightly suspicious of and resistant to "these uncontrolled powers that tend to usurp the supreme wisdom." Rather than some "mysterious effervescence," Blondel's mystical is, as Kerlin shows, a contemplative moment ingredient in the philosopher's ordinary activity.

In a general way, their mystic turn helped the figures involved in the Modernist crisis find the "breathing space" Barmann describes the early von Hügel as seeking.[48] As Talar suggests, recourse to the mystical supported their appeal against neoscholasticism's massive objectivity to what, following William James, we refer to now in a matter-of-fact way

46. Barmann, "The Modernist as Mystic," 223, n. 25, for Barmann's discussion, in terms of God as both immanent and transcendent, of what the "mystical element in personal religion" meant to von Hügel.

47. Baron Friedrich von Hügel, *The Mystical Element of Religion as Studied in Saint Catherine of Genoa and Her Friends,* 2nd ed., 2 vols. (London: Dent, 1923), I: xii.

48. Barmann, "The Modernist as Mystic," 220.

as "religious experience." Von Hügel's "mystical element" and Blondel's *la vraie et seule mystique* reached for all that had been squeezed out of Catholicism since the seventeenth century, the wider and deeper Catholicism that an overly intellectualized theology obscured. Von Hügel used the more traditional adjectival form "mystical" to designate one of three interrelated elements of Catholicism. It interacts with the historical-institutional and intellectual elements. Rather than in some extraordinary psychological phenomenon, it is in von Hügel's lifelong project of integrating these three elements that Barmann finds his mysticism.

William James' *Varieties of Religious Experience* appeared in 1902 after having been delivered at Edinburgh. In occasional vocabulary, brief engagements, and acknowledgments, William James hovers around the *Mystical Element,* especially at the beginning of volume two. One might be tempted to read the recourse of von Hügel and the others to the mystical as part of a wider turn of the century discourse of modern mysticism described by Leigh Schmidt. In the face of a determinism that threatened to engulf will by force, mysticism, precisely in its essentialism, offered James "an intellectual shield against untrammeled naturalism." But, Schmidt concludes,

> For James and those within the wider milieu of liberal Protestantism, the preserve of mysticism was only secondarily about protecting religion from its cultured despisers. It was primarily a construct formed of lacking and loss, an empty space of longing for "a heightened, intensified way of life," a search for "an *undivided whole of experience*" in an increasingly fragmented world of serialized and alienated selves [the phrases in quotation marks are from the Quaker Rufus Jones].[49]

The question of how we might position the subjects of these chapters with respect to the emerging early twentieth-century discourse of modern mysticism merges into the old and never completely resolved question about how to relate Catholic Modernists and liberal Protestants. Despite surface similarities of language, there are obvious differences between the mystical appeals of von Hügel and Bremond and the

49. Schmidt, "The Making of Modern 'Mysticism,'" 282–83 on Quietists and Quakers; 288 for mysticism as James' "intellectual shield"; 294 for Schmidt's conclusion.

mysticism of James' *Varieties.* One thinks of the role of self-renunciation or suffering for von Hügel, a cruciform love mysticism, if you will. As Hill shows, Loisy defined mysticism so broadly as to make the question difficult even to pose in his case. But, if we could pose it, Loisy against Bergson seems closest of all our subjects to Schmidt's modern mysticism. Talar suggests that Bremond sought in the "succession of mystics he studied in the pages of the *Histoire*" the sense of "God's presence and action he did not feel within himself." For Houtin, of course, Madame Bruyère as *grande mystique* had to be sick. Von Hügel and Blondel, Bremond, Loisy and Tyrrell, and the rest, they were all seekers in the time that gave us modern mysticism.

And yet they were different from Schmidt's modern mystics. As participants in a living tradition, they desired to recover a fuller and deeper Catholicism than present "rigidities" (Wilfrid Ward's term) allowed. This desire led them, especially von Hügel and Bremond, to a serious spiritual *ressourcement.* Rather than to a vacuous, universal mystic essence, they turned to particular early moderns such as Catherine and Fénelon. From Blondel this turn passed to Henri de Lubac and into one of the main streams of what Lash calls the "rich and fruitful renaissance of Catholic life, thought, and spirituality" which occurred just after mid-twentieth century.[50] In another time of seeking, a return to Modernists as mystics similarly serves us.

50. See Henri de Lubac, S.J., *Augustinianism and Modern Theology,* trans. Lancelot Sheppard (New York: Herder and Herder, 1969). The French original was published in 1965. Fénelon appears throughout the pages of this book. Lubac enlists him as one, though not a Jansenist, of the "Augustinian school," who helps to show that the "pure nature" hypothesis did not have unanimous support in the modern period. See, e.g., 284–87.

2 Mysticism and Modernism in Baron Friedrich von Hügel's Life and Thought

Lawrence F. Barmann

Whenever the name of Baron Friedrich von Hügel is mentioned, the context is nearly always that of the Modernist controversy within the Roman Catholic Church. Indeed, of the dozens of books and articles written about him in the eighty years since his death, the vast majority have had to do with his role in that controversy. Yet a serious and systematic study of his life and writings unequivocally indicates that Friedrich von Hügel was a Roman Catholic Modernist precisely because he was a Roman Catholic mystic. Should this seem questionable to someone, the cause, most likely, would be that individual's lack of a close acquaintance with the life and thought of von Hügel, or perhaps such a person's uncritical acceptance of the defamatory caricature of all so-called Modernists in Pius X's *Pascendi dominici gregis,* or even the fact that many who were called Modernists were not mystics. Or, perhaps all three! But to really understand Friedrich von Hügel one must not only study his mystical doctrine, but also the way in which his life and work were expressions of this doctrine.

Born in Florence in the early years of Pope Pius IX's long reign and into a family in which his mother was a convert from Presbyterianism and his father was only perfunctorily Catholic, the young von Hügel seems not to have found the Catholic practice which he experienced in his early years something to which he could wholeheartedly commit. When he was in his fifties and looking back on his early life in Italy, von Hügel remarked that it was the Italy of the early Renaissance and pre-Reformation period, the Italy of Dante and the Florentine Platonists, which inspired him. It was, he said, a time "yet neither Protestant nor anti-Protestant, but deeply positive and Catholic." Those early modern times, he continued, presented him with

> Men of the same general instincts and outlook as my own, but environed by the priceless boon and starting-point of a still undivided Western Christendom; Protestantism, as such continued to be felt as ever more or less unjust and sectarian; and the specifically post-Tridentine type of Catholicism, with its regimental Seminarism, its predominantly controversial spirit, its suspiciousness and timidity, persisted, however inevitable some of it may be, in its failure to win my love. Hence I had to continue the seeking and finding elsewhere, yet ever well within the great Roman Church, things more intrinsically loveable.[1]

He wrote those words in explanation of why he had decided to write a book on the pre-Reformation Saint Catherine of Genoa and mysticism. But the years between his early life and Italy and his writing *The Mystical Element of Religion* in London were indeed years of seeking and finding in Catholicism something "deeply positive and Catholic."

When Friedrich's father retired from his duties with the Austrian government, the von Hügels moved to southern England. Karl von Hügel's health was rapidly deteriorating and he decided to make one last trip to his beloved Vienna with his wife and eldest son. However, he died on the way in Brussels, leaving the eighteen-year-old Friedrich and his mother to take the body to the Austrian capital for burial.[2] While

1. Baron Friedrich von Hügel, *The Mystical Element of Religion As Studied in Saint Catherine of Genoa and Her Friends*, vol. 1, (London: Dent, 1908), v–vi. See also page 95, where he writes: "Catherine thus lived within a period which, in its depths, was already modern, but not yet broken up into seemingly final, institutionalized internecine antagonisms. And hence we can get in her a most restful and bracing pure affirmativeness, an entire absence of religious controversy, such as, of necessity, cannot be found in even such predominately interior souls as the great pre-Reformation Spanish Mystics. Her whole religion can grow and show itself as simply positive, and in rivalry and conflict with her own false self and with that alone."

2. See Lawrence Barmann, "Baron Friedrich von Hügel and Mysticism: In Pursuit of the

there Friedrich contracted typhus and was already suffering from nervous anxiety brought on by his father's death. This crisis had two results in the young von Hügel's life. One was that it left him permanently deaf and chronically subject to nervous exhaustion. The second was that he met in Vienna a Dominican priest who helped him pull his life together within the framework of a growing religious faith. The priest was Father Raymond Hocking, and it was this man, von Hügel always maintained, who first set the Baron's face toward the religious commitment and growth which became his life's primary work. Hocking did this by showing von Hügel that real Christian asceticism, patient and plodding, always based on the realities of his here and now situation, and motivated by a desire for God, was the indispensable framework for a fully developed Catholic Christian life. In a word, Christianly motivated discipline![3]

Three years after returning from Vienna von Hügel married and eventually raised three daughters. From the time of his return onward, and within the reality of his family life, he began his relentless search for God and the truth of Catholic Christianity. That search was not only intellectual, though it was indeed also impressively intellectual. But it was also a search which involved self-discipline, prayer, as frequent a use of the sacraments as was allowed a hundred years ago, and vigorous interaction with those he sensed were also serious searchers wherever they might be in their search. Gradually he came to realize that for religion to be fully developed, whether in the individual or in the *ecclesia* as a whole, it must include three distinct but integrated and interactive elements which he described as the intellectual element or philosophico-theological element, the mystical element or the prayer and sacramental dimension, and finally the historical external element or the institutional side and function of religion.[4] In the late nineteenth and early twentieth centuries, the very decades in which von Hügel began and developed his search for a deeply positive and Catholic religion, the authorities

Christian Ideal," in *Sanctity and Secularity during the Modernist Period,* ed. Lawrence Barmann and C. J. T. Talar (Brussels: Société des Bollandistes, 1999), 106–7.

3. Ibid., 107–8.

4. Von Hügel, *The Mystical Element of Religion,* 50–82.

representing the institutional element in Catholicism had become so authoritarian as to wrongly limit and nearly stifle the other two elements of religion in a systematic way, which was destructive both to individual Catholics and to the entire church. Vatican approved scholasticism had become the sole framework allowed for theological thought and writing, and any form or expression of mysticism was immediately suspect in Rome, as it had been since the Reformation and especially since the seventeenth century. The solution to this dilemma was, obviously, not to destroy the institutional element, but to try to liberate the other two elements and work toward the balanced, equal, and harmonious interaction of all three. This goal became the motive force of von Hügel's life and work.

In his early twenties von Hügel began his search in earnest, in the course of which he developed a procedural methodology which served him well for the rest of his life. The methodology was simple: read widely, and, when an author causes significant resonance, interview him by letter, or better face-to-face, and usually he did both. Some of his earliest forays were with the Jesuit Fathers at Farm Street with whom in his early years he made numerous retreats and with whom he regularly met.[5] One early encounter, which lasted nearly ten years, was with a neighbor in Hampstead, with whom he regularly walked on Hampstead Heath, arguing religious positions. The man was William George Ward. Ward, forty years von Hügel's senior, was unique among Oxford Movement converts to Catholicism, holding, for instance, positions on ecclesiastical authority and papal infallibility more extreme even than those of Pius IX.[6] While acknowledging that he was in "frank and open conflict" with Ward on most topics, von Hügel was grateful to Ward for making him think through major theological and ecclesiastical issues and developing sound evidences for his own positions.[7] Another ma-

5. This information is contained in von Hügel's *Diaries,* which are now in the von Hügel collection at St. Andrews University Library. The *Diaries* through the mid-1880s are especially indicative.

6. Wilfrid Ward, *William George Ward and the Catholic Revival* (London: Macmillan, 1893), 234–74, but especially 261–74.

7. Ibid., 365–75. Ward had asked von Hügel to write an appreciation of his father to be included in the son's biography of him, and von Hügel's generous but very frank remarks about

jor early influence on the Baron, but in a more positive direction, was Ward's fellow convert, John Henry Newman. Newman's books were especially important to the Baron, and after digesting them he went to Birmingham for several interviews with the Oratorian and soon-to-be Cardinal. He believed that the latter's *Loss and Gain* first made him "realize the intellectual might and grandeur of the Catholic position."[8] After having read the *Apologia, Anglican Difficulties,* and the *Grammar of Assent,* von Hügel told Newman that "[s]uch intellectual discipline as I have had, I owe to your books. They have, I hope, made up to me, at least somewhat, for the absence in my youthful years of any systematic training, any sympathetic and reliable teacher."[9]

In the 1880s and 1890s the von Hügels often traveled on the continent, and frequently spent the winters in the south of France or in Rome. In Paris in 1884, the Baron first met Abbé Louis Duchesne whose critical historical work influenced him for the rest of his life.[10] And in that same year he also met for the first time Abbé Henri Huvelin whose counsels and spiritual direction set von Hügel firmly on the road which resulted in the extraordinary achievement of his own integrated life and his important writings. Five years before his own death von Hügel remarked of Huvelin in a lecture he gave in Oxford that "I owe more to this Frenchman than to any other man I have ever known in the flesh."[11]

Ward's influence on himself are found there. See also Friedrich von Hügel, "Christianity and the Supernatural," in *Essays and Addresses on the Philosophy of Religion* (London: Dent, 1921), 280. In this address, which von Hügel gave at Oxford in 1920, he again speaks of Ward's influence on him.

8. Von Hügel to H. I. D. Ryder, 18 August 1890, Birmingham Oratory Archives (BOA), VC 20.

9. Von Hügel to J. H. Newman, 13 December 1874, BOA, VC 20. In the Preface to his *Mystical Element of Religion* (xv) von Hügel wrote: "But further back than all the living writers and friends lies the stimulation and help of him who was later to become Cardinal Newman. It was he who first taught me to glory in my appurtenance to the Catholic and Roman Church, and to conceive this my inheritance in a large and historical manner, as a slow growth across the centuries, with an innate affinity to, and eventual incorporation of, all the good and true to be found mixed up with error and with evil in this chequered, difficult but rich world and life in which this living organism moves and expands."

10. Friedrich von Hügel, "Louis Duchesne," *The Times Literary Supplement* 1062 (25 May 1922): 342.

11. Friedrich von Hügel, "Christianity and the Supernatural," 286.

Something of what he owed to Huvelin can be gathered from the notes von Hügel took from his multiple interviews with this saintly priest of Saint Augustine's church in Paris.[12] Basically, Huvelin helped him free himself from fear of his own vigorous and impetuous personality in order to work more effectively with God's grace. Huvelin immediately recognized in von Hügel a rare individual who, like himself, needed to combine a critical intellect with full church commitment. He saw that von Hügel could never fit into the mold which late nineteenth-century Catholicism sought to impose. So he showed the younger man how to take less seriously the scholastic strictures and dicta emanating from Rome, indicating that nineteenth-century scholasticism dealt with formulae, not reality, and that scholastic writers failed to grasp that all real life is ultimately unanalysable. Since contemporary Catholic orthodoxy was formed in scholastic formulae, von Hügel was told not to aim at orthodoxy as a thing in itself. He would aim, rather, at conscientiousness in his pursuit of truth because conscience *always* takes precedence over orthodoxy. Orthodoxy's responsibility is to square itself with truth. And in many other ways Huvelin helped von Hügel grow spiritually with his insights on prayer, relationships with others, religious practice, asceticism, and calmness or peacefulness of spirit.

During the 1870s and 1880s von Hügel was increasingly coming to realize the importance for himself of understanding both the Old and New Testaments. He had been reading the latter in its original Greek since the early seventies, and in the eighties he began a serious and prolonged study of Hebrew with several scholars, until he was reading the Old Testament in its original language as well.[13] As the issues of biblical inspiration and the authenticity of various biblical texts increasingly exercised Catholic biblical scholars, von Hügel was following these developments in most of the major European languages. From 1894 to

12. When Bernard Holland edited von Hügel's *Selected Letters* in 1927, he published the original French of *most* of these notes. *Baron Friedrich von Hügel. Selected Letters 1896–1924*, ed. Bernard Holland (London, Dent, 1927). The *full* text, taken from von Hügel's manuscript, was only published fifty years later by James Kelly, "The Abbé Huvelin's Counsels to Baron Friedrich von Hügel," *Bijdragen Tijdschrift voor Filosofie en Theologie* 39 (1978): 59–69.

13. Lawrence Barmann, *Baron Friedrich von Hügel and the Modernist Crisis in England* (Cambridge: Cambridge University Press, 1972), 11–13.

1895 he even published a series of articles in the *Dublin Review* on "The Church and the Bible: The Two Stages of Their Inter-Relation," which was an effort to show that Leo XIII's *Providentissimus Deus* did not necessarily preclude, as most commentators believed, a serious science of the Bible as distinguished from its dogmatic and devotional use.[14]

Although von Hügel had been reading Alfred Loisy's biblical studies for several years, he had only met the scholar in October of 1893, and recognized how important Loisy's work could be for the Church. But by the time that *Providentissimus Deus* was published in November 1893 Loisy was already in trouble with Cardinal Richard of Paris who would eventually get Rome to condemn him as well. Over the next decade and a half von Hügel was not an uncritical evaluator of Loisy's work, but he fought strenuously, until Loisy's excommunication in 1908, for the right of the Frenchman to pursue his scholarly work on the Bible.[15]

The von Hügels lived in Hampstead until 1903, and they were a prominent family in that community of prominent and artistic Londoners. The Protestant publisher of *The Hampstead Annual*, Sydney Mayle, invited von Hügel to write an article on one of the great Catholic mystics. He agreed, and the result was a fifteen-page article on Saint Catherine of Genoa that, in the course of the next ten years, evolved into the two-volume *Mystical Element of Religion*.[16] In writing the article von Hügel clarified for himself his ideas on mysticism and ran them by his newly found and mystical-minded friend Father George Tyrrell, S.J.[17] Von Hügel's ideas on spiritual purification agreed with the actual practice of the great mystics rather than with most contemporary and ecclesiastically approved mystical theory, and through his discussions with Tyrrell he gained confidence in his own positions. He was also concerned to show that there was no necessary connection in the lives of various mystics, and especially that of Saint Catherine of Genoa, between their physi-

14. Friedrich von Hügel, "The Church and the Bible: The Two Stages of Their Inter-Relation," *The Dublin Review*, vols. CXV–CXVII, nos. 231, 233, and 235 (October 1894; April and October 1895): 313–41, 306–37, and 273–304.

15. Barmann, *Baron Friedrich von Hügel and the Modernist Crisis*, 38–53, 79–137, and 275–304.

16. Von Hügel to George Tyrrell, 21 November 1898, *Selected Letters*, 74–76.

17. Von Hügel to George Tyrrell, 26 September 1898, *Selected Letters*, 71–74. See also von Hügel's *Diaries* from September 27 to October 25, 1898.

cal and psychic health problems and the moral/spiritual characters of their teachings. From a study of the sources for Catherine of Genoa's life, he had concluded that what her fifteenth-century contemporaries had termed miraculous in her life was due in fact to her suffering from hysteria.[18] But in spite of this she was a genuine Catholic mystic and saint.

As von Hügel began his work on the larger study of mysticism, his two closest intellectual friends, Loisy and Tyrrell, were coming under increasing scrutiny for their ideas, and, eventually, condemnation and excommunication from Rome. To save these two men and their work for the Church and its future, as well as to get his own book published without Roman condemnation, became his dominant effort and tension of these years. By December of 1901, he had finished what would be the first volume of the published work and was set to finish the second volume within the next year, he hoped. He told Tyrrell that

> I can't help hoping now, more strongly than at first, that the result of the whole will be a living organism, something that will be able to enter into other minds and hearts, and grow and bring fruit there. Certainly the effect upon myself is being considerable: I have become a good bit more of a person, please God of the right, the spiritual-humble sort, by battling and toiling with and in and over these great realities and problems.[19]

By the following June, however, he was telling Tyrrell that he was no born writer like Tyrrell was, that his health was always precarious, and "my strength goes in trying to console and sustain friends scattered about over the face of Europe." And, he continued, "this again, I should not mind or complain of, still I want badly to express myself, in my

18. Von Hügel to George Tyrrell, 3 October 1898, in M. D. Petre, *Von Hügel and Tyrrell: The Story of a Friendship* (London: Dent, 1937), 45–46. See also, Barmann, "Baron Friedrich von Hügel and Mysticism," 120–26. In 1909 von Hügel sent a letter to William James, telling him what he liked and disliked about the latter's *The Varieties of Religious Experience,* and remarking that James' first chapter was "a truly magnificent *attacco;* I have often wished that it might appear as a separate booklet for every word tells, every word is weighty and much wanted in these our nerve-racked unwisely introspective times." Von Hügel to William James, 10 May 1909, in J. L. Adams, "Letter from Friedrich von Hügel to William James," in *Downside Review* 98 (1980): 228.

19. Von Hügel to George Tyrrell, 18–20 December 1901, British Library (BL), MSS 44927.175.

writings, if only once, and as well as I can. But I cannot do both, attend to my friends *and* my book."[20]

Nevertheless, he did do both, and at enormous personal cost. The book was ready for the publisher late in 1908, more than a year after the publication of *Pascendi dominici gregis*; and during those same years of its writing no single individual did more on multiple fronts to save progressive historical and theological thinkers for the Catholic Church than Friedrich von Hügel. The Baron's friends and allies in the struggle were not only Roman Catholics, but religious-minded men of various ecclesiastical commitments. And a group of these, all high-church Anglican clerics, asked him to give a paper early in 1904. This group called themselves the Twelve Silent Men, although the gathering numbered fifteen when von Hügel addressed them on the evening of January 28, 1904.[21] He called his paper "Official Authority and Living Religion," and it articulated with calm detachment why it is appropriate to call von Hügel both a Modernist and a mystic, for it was in fact highly autobiographical.

He began this address by noting that religious warfare in the Western world of the twentieth century was no longer between Protestant and Catholic, nor theist and atheist. Rather, it was within historical, institutional Christianity, and between the officials of the institutions and loyal members of those same churches who realized that many of their doctrines needed re-thinking and restatement in light of the application of historico-critical methodology applied to their sources, the Bible and church tradition. There is conflict here, von Hügel says, because "the official *as such* speaks, thinks and acts, as the organ and expression of the corporate speech, thought and action."[22] The corporation, con-

20. Von Hügel to George Tyrrell, 4 June 1902, BL, MSS 44928.13.

21. Von Hügel, *Diaries*, 28 January 1904: "Worked hard at Address . . . In aft. Finished up writing fair of Address 'Official Authority & Living Religion'. By tube to Bond St. Walked to Fischer's Hotel, Clifford St. Dined there w. the 'XII Silent Men'. Revd Mr. Shaw-Stewart, host; A. L. Lilley sat next to me. About 15 persons besides me, at meeting afterwards. *Read them the Address I had composed for them, on 'Official Authority & Living Religion'.* Walked back home,—A. L. Lilley with me as far as Marble Arch."

22. Baron Friedrich von Hügel, "Official Authority and Living Religion," in *Essays and Addresses on the Philosophy of Religion*, second series, (London: Dent, 1926), 3–23. All other quotations from this address are from these pages and will not be individually cited.

sidered here analogously, is the institutional Church. And the average educated Christian, to the extent that he truly and deeply lives the life of the mind and spirit, even if only partially and intermittently, does not feel, think, will and act, suffer, love and rejoice, "in the same manner, with the same form and categories, as officialdom seems to do and to direct him to do." So there is a dichotomy here between the officials of a church and the serious Christian members of that church. And to the latter the dichotomy seems to be between reality and unreality.

Seven characteristics, von Hügel says, ever mark all such a Christian's deepest moments and efforts, and seven contrary peculiarities ever characterize official acts as such. First, whenever such a Christian with focus and deep self-possession "thinks, wills; prays, adores; suffers, rejoices; produces: *that* act, *that* state, *that* result, *that* very man, are truly *new* and original." They are new not only in the sense of being new for that individual, in that time and place, but new and unique in countless other ways, von Hügel says. And if this newness is at all creative and fruitful, it will be a revelation not of Time but of Eternity. "Or, at least, it will be a duration of mutually interpenetrative experiences, rather than a clear succession of experiences in time, where one element is made to exclude the other."[23] Authority, on the other hand, will necessarily represent the past, that which has already been.

Second, according to von Hügel, in such moments of living religious effort the individual Christian will feel lonely and isolated, even isolated from his own average thoughts and moments as well as from the average majority of men. And in this will be a certain exhilaration. But officialdom always necessarily insists on the majority, the average. It cannot help being essentially philistine.

23. The Baron's expression here seems to owe something to his reading of Henri Bergson's *Essai sur les donnés immédiates de la conscience*. In October 1900, he wrote to Tyrrell that he had "read and digested it all with the deepest attention, profit and gratitude. I doubt whether I have ever read an equal number of pages which have taught me more. I think you too will find that he will help further clear your mind in an extraordinary degree. But do not please shy at the rather dry and at first sight but slightly important chapter I: it is really the absolutely necessary foundation for the two delightful chapters which follow." Von Hügel to Tyrrell, 8 October 1900, BL, MSS 44927.139. And in the Preface to his *Mystical Element of Religion* von Hügel writes: "Among present-day French writers, my book owes most to . . . and to M. Henri Bergson's *Essai sur les donnés immédiatges de la Conscience*" (xv).

In such moments of really intense spiritual activity the focused Christian will seem to himself to be passive, merely yielding to suffering or pain or resisting bad habits and self-seeking. And this activity is ultimately Christ's "in its very possibility, occasion, actuality, truth, strength and fruitfulness." Authority, however, insists on a true passivity, in which it acts on the believer, or allows him activity only to make room for authority to act on him.

The Baron's fourth characteristic of a Christian's deepest moments and most intense life is that he "necessarily risks and dares much, and is truly conscious of such risking." Everything worthwhile in life requires risk, he says, and "so every truly noble life is noble largely through its having courageously risked all risks necessary to its own expansion, growth and fruitfulness; for these latter are the only true safety attainable by man here below." Authority insists on eliminating risk as much as possible, emphasizing external, static, immediate, though weakening safeties which nearly inevitably lead to stagnation and sterility.

Another characteristic of the Christian in his deepest moments is his awareness that his life is a constant search for objective truth, and in this awareness he finds security. Also he is aware of an ever-growing purity of disposition and intention on his part, and a growing attempt to become and to be all that he knows. He is also aware that his progress toward this goal is never ending, so his focus is primarily on his search rather than on the goal. Not so with Authority, which dwells upon the end rather than the means, upon objective truth rather than subjective truthfulness. It sees truth "as something static, readily transferable, identical with certain formularies—an orthodoxy, a thing."

The sixth characteristic of this deeply living Christian is to find behind and through the phenomenal world of our lives the beauty, truth, goodness and spirit which is God. This is attainable only by one's "concentration, prayer, suffering, and self-dedication," using certain times, places, rites, and forms as bridges to "graces which it may and can refuse; which it can and ought to meet and utilize." Official Authority tends to see beauty, truth, and goodness in the phenomenal world as merely phenomena alongside phenomenal ugliness, error, and evil. And the former are found in some one particular place and enclosure.

It is as though a vertical, geological conception had here been replaced by a horizontal geographical outlook; and the consequent need of digging down in our investigations, by a simple task of searching for what lies on the surface of life."

The final characteristic of von Hügel's seven, and one that he sees as the consequence of the previous six, is an optimism in and through pessimism. No matter how poor and shabby such a vibrant Christian senses his own life to be and the life of the world generally, he also realizes that through it all, both in his own life and in the whole world, God's own Spirit is pushing and growing and working. Official Authority is, on the contrary, always optimistic, "at least as regards its own action and the results of this action, past, present, and future."

Summarizing the seven individual characteristics and their corporate opposites, von Hügel wrote:

> In a word, the soul at its deepest is ever profoundly original, isolated, active, daring, interior, penetrative, and superficially pessimist; it moves through suffering on to joy. And official Authority is, as such, ever repetitive of something past and gone; is the voice of the average thoughts of the many; aims at limiting the action of its subjects to a passive reception and more or less mechanical execution of its commands; is essentially timid; cares necessarily more for the outward appearance and material output, than for the interior disposition and form of the soul's activity; maps out the very phenomenal world into visible, mutually exclusive regions of spiritual light and darkness; and is in so far ever unreal, as it cannot but absolutely disallow, or must at least minimise as much as possible, all even preliminary present sins, pains and perplexities—at least those of its own creation.

Given that analysis of the conflict between the most deep and vigorous Christians with the official church authorities, it would seem obvious that Christians should simply "throw all such social, institutional, official Authority overboard" and get on with their own spiritual growth. But no, von Hügel insists that such "a rejection would be an all the more dangerous mistake, as it would readily look, and at first feel, like an act of manly simplification and spiritual interiorisation." He then goes back over the seven positions taken by authorities which he had juxtaposed to the characteristics of the fully alive and growing Christian, and he shows how in each of these seemingly negative positions there also exists a dimension which is both necessary for the strenuous soul, and, in fact, necessary for the Church as a whole.

> But, above all, and throughout all these seven points, it is clear that Offical-ism, of some kind or degree, is inevitable if we would make a reasonable, continuous provision for applying the motive force and light of the leading, stimulating, renovating few to the dull, average, more or less automatic many—the few highest thoughts, volitions and experiences of any one man to the multitude of his average experience; and the predominant dispositions and actions of the few whose religious life is almost entirely first-hand to the multitude of men whose religion is average in its attainments. And such relation is not by any means only necessary for those many thoughts and many men; it is at least as, though differently, necessary for those few who gain from such communication that uniquely noble, creaturely sense of each requiring and supplementing the other. For only then shall we avoid a gnostic, esoteric, "Palace of Art" infatuation, and the loss of that greatest glory of Christianity, the corporate spirit, the love of universal brotherhood, the sense of the indestructible, though most easily deniable, interdependence of all times and races, gifts and activities of life, the supremacy of Love over knowledge, and of Action over speculation.

He then went on to argue that in the whole of human history some form or other of religious organization has prevailed, and done so necessarily. And, he says, it can be shown historically "how *spiritually beneficent* is some kind and degree of organization and officiality, or rather how the fuller and fullest interior life not only can thrive in, but seems actually to require, and itself to occasion, a vigorous, definite Church organization." In proof he cites Jesus, Saint Paul, Clement of Alexandria and Origen, Saint Francis of Assisi, Saint John of the Cross, and Saint Teresa of Avila.

But history also shows, he says, that truly religious men have tried consistently to show "to all not beyond the reach of learning, that there are certain profound dangers and difficulties attendant upon all officialdom; certain readily, all but inevitable, forgotten laws and limits of its efficacious exercise." These laws, he says, are fundamentally two, and they are reinforced by "two great historico-critical conclusions."

The first law is that the official organization and authority of any religious society is only a part, even if a necessary part, of a dynamic whole. And that whole includes the "new and daring (if but faithful, reverent, and loving) outgoing of the discoverer and investigator" who is also a necessary part of the whole. The second of the two laws is that "official organisation and Authority are ever the means, necessary means, of life; means, not ends; of life, not of death."

Historical criticism of the Bible has resulted in establishing several issues which are important to any discussion of official authority within the Church. It has shown that church organization and officialdom as we know it are not the direct and deliberate creation of Jesus himself. Von Hügel writes:

> Now this conclusion necessarily involves the recognition that all and every officialdom beyond that humble brotherhood, so simply trained, organised and sent out by Him, can but go back germinally and not formally and materially to Him, somewhat as the visible universe itself was germinally created by God in the beginning, and not in the state or form in which we now see it.

This realization should result in understanding that all contemporary Christian churches go far beyond the Gospel confraternity both in structural organization and systematic creed. So any pursuit of a *pure* Christianity is the pursuit of a chimera. So, says von Hügel, we all have always the need "to introduce width, elasticity, and a noble humanity into our conception of the Church."

His second conclusion from biblical criticism has to do with the genuinely human dimension of Jesus' knowledge, and this means that this knowledge was not "exempt from mental growth, struggle, obscurity; from dim and partially mistaken gropings and guesses." So if Jesus was fully human, and without denying his divinity, he had to have limited knowledge. And so, concludes the Baron, "it is truly impossible that theologians, or indeed Church Authority generally, should have an inerrancy higher, or more extensive in degree or kind, than Our Lord's; or, rather, that He should be less infallible than they."

Sometime after delivering this address, von Hügel sent a typed copy to Tyrrell with a note, telling him that he was enclosing "my typed Paper on 'Official Authority' as you might care to read it. I did it as an act of faith and self elucidation, at the height of the crisis, and read it to

Lilley's 'XII Silent Men'. Let me have it back, in due course please."[24] On March 20, 1904, Tyrrell wrote to the Baron about this paper:

Your paper on "Official Authority" seems to me most satisfying & constructive; but I wonder how much the 12 masked conspirators understood of it. It requires awful concentration of attention & it was only in making a careful synopsis of it, that I really seized its full import. *I* should have put all that into 300 8vo pp. & sold it for 5/- nett; & people would have said it was overcrowded & obscure. *For you* each word is chosen & placed with full explicit consciousness & meaning. But what audience will appreciate that? Not even the Cherubim or Seraphim. Even for purposes of reading & study I think you might consider the average man a little more. It was the same with your most wonderful Synthetic paper which you stuffed like a light sausage. Solid, liquid, gas—are the three forms in which thoughts can be presented; the last for an audience; the second for a book; the first for an archangel in retreat. I don't think anything has helped & satisfied me so much as this last paper of yours, & I shall be doling out bits of it for years to come according as it sinks into my mind & bears fruit there.[25]

This brief summary has tried to indicate the harmonious growth of both the mystical and Modernist dimensions of Baron von Hügel's life during his first fifty years. His mystical dimension necessitated his de facto role in the Modernist crisis within a church structurally closed at that time to so much of God's truth, beauty, and goodness in the created world of man's intellectual endeavors. The fullest expressions of his ideas on the mystical dimension of an actively involved Christian's life are, of course, contained in his two-volume *The Mystical Element of Religion,* which has been called recently "one of the masterpieces of the modern study of mysticism."[26] But one should note that von Hügel's address to the twelve Silent Men was written and delivered when the manuscript of his book was almost entirely complete. The book aimed at demonstrating how the mystical dimension of a committed Chris-

24. Von Hügel to George Tyrrell, n.d., BL, MSS 44929.146. This is a letter fragment, undated, which the British Library includes with the letters of 1906. However, since Tyrrell's response to it is dated 20 March 1904, this letter of von Hügel's had to be from between 28 January 1904 and 20 March 1904.

25. Tyrrell to von Hügel, 20 March 1904, BL, MSS 44928.183–84.

26. Bernard McGinn, *The Foundations of Mysticism* (New York: Crossroad Publishing Company, 1991), 293.

tian's life was one of the three necessary dimensions of such a life; while the address was aimed primarily at demonstrating that the limitations of church officialdom were, on the one hand, mostly in opposition to the growth of this mystical dimension but, on the other hand, in some partial way necessary to its full fruitfulness. This dilemma was well demonstrated in the Baron's own life, as he struggled to save what was best in critical biblical studies and contemporary theology for the Church while being consistently opposed by church authorities who thought they had nothing to learn from modern intellectual developments. This opposition was manifest in von Hügel's mystical theories. He believed that some degree of mysticism, no matter how rudimentary and tentative, was a constitutive part of *every* serious Christian's life. His writings not only consistently reflect this implicitly, but he also made this explicit in a letter to his friend Abbot Cuthbert Butler of Downside Abbey.[27] And this very idea itself went against the mystical theory currently acceptable at the Vatican, though, as he told Butler, it was part of an older, classical Catholic tradition. From the perspective of nearly a century, one can see that it was von Hügel, unlike so many others, both Modernists and anti-Modernist church authorities, who never lost his balance as a Catholic. And he has still much to teach serious Catholics and Christians generally in today's crises within the churches.

27. Von Hügel to Cuthbert Butler, 4 July 1911, Downside Abbey Archives, von Hügel MSS.

3 Prayer at Twilight

Henri Bremond's *Apologie pour Fénelon*

C. J. T. Talar

Nineteenth-century criticism possessed all the data necessary for judging soundly Fénelon's humanism and his spirituality. But the prejudices were tenacious and erudition could make no headway against them. Researchers turned less toward the study of a thought than toward the history of a conflict. With rare exceptions, each was interested in the duel between the two bishops, at the risk of fixing them in oversimplified postures; most often, Fénelon was the angel of darkness.[1]

In March 1699 the papal brief *Cum alias* condemned twenty-three propositions extracted from the *Explication des Maximes des Saints sur la Vie intérieure*, published by François Fénelon (1651–1715) in 1697. It is generally thought that political pressure applied by Louis XIV accomplished what the serial polemics of Jacques-Bénigne Bossuet (1627–1704) and the efforts of his namesake nephew installed at Rome could not. The commission of cardinals charged with examining the book had split evenly—the pope's brief decided the matter. Mysticism, already in decline by the end of the seventeenth century and the object of suspicion, thereafter largely disappeared from the public arena.[2] Not so Fé-

1. Jeanne-Lydie Goré, *L'itinéraire de Fénelon: Humanisme et Spiritualité* (Paris: Presses Universitaires de France, 1957), 15.

2. Louis Cognet entitled his study of the Quietist controversy, *La crépuscule des mystiques* (Paris: Desclée, 1995).

nelon, however. Though the vanquished party, and exiled to his diocese of Cambrai, his reputation endured throughout the next century.

In the nineteenth century, by contrast, Bossuet's star was in the ascendant in both ecclesiastical circles and the academy. And in both was manifest a corresponding tendency to denigrate Fénelon. In 1895, writing in the *Revue du clergé français,* Abbé Delfour lamented the severity with which Bossuet's rival was treated—"as if admiration for one great man necessarily implied the violent dislike of another!"[3] In the same year L. Boutié reviewed in *Études* the charges leveled against Fénelon by several recent critics, summing those up as an unreal, impractical spirit; ardent political ambitions fed by egoistic passion; and a lack of sincerity manifested in his submission to the decree that condemned the *Maximes des Saints.*[4] Although Boutié supplied counterfactuals to these alleged defects of character, he was clearly swimming against the current. As was anyone who wished to restore the fortunes of mysticism.

In the French secular university, mysticism had long since acquired a name and a face: Quietism and Madame Guyon. Or faces really: she and Fénelon were considered mysticism's last serious representatives. And, from the perspective of the medical model then highly influential, they represented the pathological states that were judged the source of mystical experiences. In the estimation of Ferdinand Brunetière, had Guyon lived in the nineteenth century, her confinement would have been in the Salpêtrière rather than the Bastille, her diagnosis religious monomania rather than heterodox spirituality.[5] Self-deceiving, she was

3. Abbé Delfour, "Le procès de Fénelon," *Revue du clergé français* 5 (1895): 214–28, at 214.

4. L. Boutié, "Fénelon: D'après quelques critiques contemporains," *Études* 66 (1895): 542–69. Boutié subsequently enlarged upon this defense, publishing *Fénelon* (Paris: Victor Retaux, 1899).

5. Ferdinand Brunetière, "La querelle du quiétisme," appeared originally in the *Revue de Deux Mondes* (15 August 1881), reprinted in his *Études critiques sur l'histoire de la littérature française* 2 [1882] (Paris: Librairie Hachette, 1922), 53. Brunetière was one of the critics singled out by Boutié in his article and Bremond would later signal this article as marking "a cardinal date" in the history of Fénelon's reception. "If eloquence could win such battles, the Fénelonians would be vanquished." See Henri Bremond, *Apologie pour Fénelon* (Paris: Perrin, 1910), 197. On Brunetière, see John Clark, *La Pensée de Ferdinand Brunetière* (Paris: Librairie Nizet, 1954) and Alain Archidec, *Ferdinand Brunetière ou la rage de croire,* 2 vols. (diss., L'Université d'Aix-en-Provence, 1974).

also adept at deceiving others: one of the complaints brought against Fénelon was his inability to admit that he had been taken in, for a period of years, by this woman.[6] Thus, in the academy mysticism, pathology, and esotericism formed an iron triangle—to retrieve Émile Poulat's characterization.

Already, at the time of the Modernist crisis, there are signs within the academy that this configuration is being pried open, signs of a sense that "these limits were also a limitation, and beyond those, there was not only the void and the unknowable, but a strange, unsettling human world, transcending the rules and norms that had currency among enlightened minds."[7] The first stirrings of such change can be detected in the Sorbonne thesis of Édouard Récéjac, a former priest who challenged the limits of a positivist reason with his analysis of mystical intuition.[8] As an inaugural date for a revaluation of mysticism within the academy, however, Poulat proposes a communication presented at the Société française de philosophie in 1905 by Henri Delacroix on the development of mystical states in Saint Teresa of Avila.[9] Three years later, in his *Études d'histoire et de psychologie du mysticisme,* Delacroix expanded his interests to include considerable material on Madame Guyon, in which he takes her claims to mystical experiences seriously, and he presents Fénelon as her faithful, though not uncritical, disciple.[10]

On the Catholic side, Bossuet's characterization of mysticism as an extraordinary phenomenon, province of an elite, yet held sway. Though mystical experience could not be denied, forming as it did part of the accepted tradition of the Church, still there was the sense that it needed to be kept under surveillance, subject to theological scrutiny and supervi-

6. Ferdinand Brunetière, "Fénelon," in *Grande Encyclopédie* XVII (1893) and reprinted in *Études critiques* 2, 305–34.

7. Émile Poulat, *L'Université devant la mystique* (Paris: Éditions Salvator, 1999), 9. See also his *Critique et mystique* (Paris: Le Centurion, 1984), ch. 8.

8. E. Récéjac, *Essai sur les fondements de la connaissance mystique* (Paris: Félix Alcan, 1897). *Essay on the Bases of the Mystic Knowledge,* English trans. Sara Carr Upton (New York: Scribner's, 1899).

9. Poulat, *L'Université devant la mystique,* 26–27.

10. Henri Delacroix, *Études d'histoire et de psychologie du mysticisme. Les grands mystiques chrétiens* (Paris: Félix Alcan, 1908). "Fénelon can be profitably studied only after Mme Guyon and in his relationship with Mme Guyon," see note at 188.

sion. Certainly, mystical experience continued within Catholicism but it was largely confined to convent and cloister and so remained for the most part hidden, a marginal phenomenon. Roughly parallel in time to the renewal of scholarly interest in mysticism that emerged within the academy, however, there are signs of a reengagement with mystics and their experiences among Catholic scholars. In 1901 appeared Auguste Poulain's *Des grâces d'oraison,* which would go through multiple editions and be translated into a number of other languages, establishing itself as something of a classic. Poulain's background was scientific, and he positioned his study as one of close observation of the phenomena of mysticism, especially among modern mystics, rather than a work of theoretical interpretation. His emphasis on extraordinary phenomena as reflective of mystical states, and the conviction that their presence is confined to a rather small elite, stand in fundamental continuity with Bossuet's views. The perspective on Quietism is also that of Bossuet, with corresponding severity toward Madame Guyon and treatment of Fénelon's errors.[11]

Moreover, the fin-de-siècle association of mysticism with pathology surfaces among Catholics as well. In the pages of *L'Ami du clergé* Fénelon could be stigmatized as "neurasthenic"—this alleged "infirmity of temperament" providing the key to understanding the "inconsistencies in his character" and his conduct in his friendships.[12] It would not be until 1910 that Fénelon's fortunes really began to change significantly among Catholics, due in significant measure to the work of Henri Bremond.[13]

Bremond's initial foray into the famous controversy between Bossuet and Fénelon assumed the form of a review of Albert Deplanque's *Fénelon et la doctrine de l'amour* pur and arrived at conclusions notably

11. Auguste Poulain, *Des grâces d'oraison. Traité de théologie mystique* [1901] (Paris: Gabriel Beauchesne, 1909). *The Graces of Interior Prayer. A Treatise on Mystical Theology,* English trans. Leonora Yorke Smith (London: Kegan Paul, Trench, Trübner, 1910). See especially ch. 27.

12. Review of Albert Delplanque, *Fénelon et la doctrine de l'amour pur,* in *L'Ami du clergé* 31 (1909): 1031–34, at 1032.

13. Goré, *L'itinéraire de Fénelon,* 20. Michael de la Bedoyère judged Bremond's *Apologie pour Fénelon* "the most intelligent modern work on Fénelon." *The Archbishop and the Lady* (New York: Pantheon, 1956), 92.

different from those reached in *L'Ami du clergé.* While Bremond did not place Delplanque within the ranks of "the modern Bossuetists" (though he was reckoned their ally), they were held to treat Fénelon with so blatant an injustice that Bremond regarded it "a duty to dispute them."[14] He did not long delay in fulfilling that responsibility. The following month the first of the articles "Pro Fenelone" appeared in the *Annales de philosophie chrétienne;*[15] they would form the basis of his *Apologie pour Fénelon* (1910).

Bremond's *Fénelon*

Though righting an imbalance and addressing an injustice where Fénelon's memory was concerned formed part of Bremond's overtly stated motives, his work on the archbishop must be seen in the larger context of his involvement in the Modernist movement and set in a larger framework of his monumental *Histoire littéraire du sentiment religieux.*

Although not himself a figure central to Modernism, Bremond maintained contact with many who were. He corresponded extensively with Maurice Blondel,[16] had an enduring friendship with Alfred Loisy,[17] knew well both Friedrich von Hügel[18] and Maude Petre, and

14. Henri Bremond, "Fénelon et la critique psychologique," in *Annales de philosophie chrétienne* 9 n.s. (October 1909–March 1910): 144–62, at 162. This review article appeared in November 1909.

15. Bremond published "Pro Fenelone" in five parts: *Annales de philosophie chrétienne* 9 (December 1909): 225–44; (January 1910): 337–71; (February 1910): 472–518; (March 1910): 593–635; and 10 (April 1910): 20–53.

16. The annotated correspondence between Bremond and Blondel over 1897 to 1933 covers three volumes. *Henri Bremond-Maurice Blondel. Correspondance,* ed. André Blanchet (Paris: Aubier-Montaigne, 1970–1971).

17. On Bremond's relations with Loisy see Émile Goichot, *Alfred Loisy et ses amis* (Paris: Cerf, 2002). Also Henri Bernard-Maitre, "A propos de 'L'Histoire littéraire du Sentiment religieux': Une correspondance de Bremond avec Loisy (1924–1929)," *Revue d'ascétique et de mystique* 45 (1969): 161–89.

18. Émile Goichot has published and annotated the correspondence between Bremond and von Hügel. See "En marge de la crise moderniste: La correspondance Bremond-von Hügel," *Revue des sciences religieuses* 48 (1974): 209–34; 49 (1975): 202–33; 53 (1979): 124–46. In the controversy that surfaced between Blondel and Loisy over the latter's *L'Évangile et l'Église* (1902), Bremond lent indirect support to Loisy through his assistance to von Hügel in his published intervention. See René Marlé, *Au coeur de la crise moderniste* (Paris: Aubier-

had close relations with George Tyrrell.[19] Indeed, the circumstances surrounding the latter's death created difficulties for Bremond with the Vatican. Put briefly, Tyrrell had incurred "minor" excommunication (deprivation of the sacraments but not exclusion from the Catholic community) over the temper of his writings. Dying of Bright's disease, he received absolution upon his expressed repentance for his sins, but made no retraction of what he had written. Absent such retraction, the local ordinary, Bishop Peter Amigo, refused permission for a Catholic funeral. On July 21, 1909, Tyrrell was buried in the Anglican churchyard at Storrington, accompanied by prayer and a funeral speech given by Bremond. In response, he was forbidden by Amigo to say Mass, a measure shortly confirmed at Rome by Cardinal Merry del Val. Bremond ultimately submitted and by the following November his right to celebrate Mass was restored.

When one recalls that Bremond's initial article on Fénelon appeared that same November, followed over the next several months by those that formed "Pro Fenelone," it is less than surprising that Fénelon's own submission and the circumstances surrounding it should have been very much on Bremond's mind.[20] So too would Fénelon's loyal refusal to disavow Madame Guyon in face of Bossuet's denunciations.[21] The parallels with Bremond's situation are drawn by Alastair Guinan:

Montaigne, 1960). Bremond's direct support took the form of his pseudonymous *Un clerc qui n'a pas trahi. Alfred Loisy d'après ses Mémoires* [1931] that he published under the name Sylvain Leblanc. (See Émile Poulat, *Une oeuvre clandestine d'Henri Bremond* [Roma: Edizioni di Storia e Letteratura, 1972].) In it Bremond distinguished between Loisy's "dogmatic faith" and his "mystical faith."

19. See Alfred Loisy, *George Tyrrell et Henri Bremond* (Paris: Émile Nourry, 1936). André Blanchet's biography, *Henri Bremond 1865–1904* (Paris: Aubier-Montaigne, 1975), unfortunately unfinished, sheds light on Bremond's relations with Petre and Tyrrell over the period it treats.

20. In a postcard dated 8 August 1909 written to Alfred Leslie Lilley, Bremond apprised him of the suspension and characterizes his answer as "half-fenelonian, half voltarian." See Alec Vidler, *A Variety of Catholic Modernists* (Cambridge: Cambridge University Press, 1970), 43.

21. "To disown a friend against whom the powerful are determinedly ranged . . . is a way of acting. Saint Peter had not invented it. It has currency still today." Bremond, *Apologie pour Fénelon,* 30. Goichot draws attention to this passage in explicitly remarking the parallel between Bremond's refusal to disown Tyrrell at his death and Fénelon's conduct in relation to Guyon. Émile Goichot, "Une très haute, très séduisante, une fatale figure. Bremond et madame Guyon," in *Madame Guyon* (Grenoble: Jérôme Millon, 1997), 173–89, at 176–77.

It was in the year following the Tyrrell affair that M. Brémond [*sic*] published his *Apologie pour Fénelon,* and it is not surprising if we discern in that noble defence of a misunderstood man a tendency to disparage the limitations of the official mind as represented by Bossuet. The Bishop of Meaux is an outstanding figure in the history of the French Church, and a man possessed, moreover, of real genius; yet in some degree he shared with Peter Amigo the temperament of one who sees in those who are in disagreement with him only a *garden enclosed,* to which he has lost the key.[22]

The year 1910 thus marks a nodal point in Bremond's personal journey: surrounding the death of Tyrrell was the failure of Modernism, and Bremond's decision to remain in the church, as well as the beginnings of the vast undertaking that would emerge as the eleven volumes of the *Histoire littéraire du sentiment religieux.*

For the rest of Bremond's life, Fénelon always stood in the background of his published work. The publication of Bremond's *Sainte Chantal* in 1912 already presages concerns that will mark the initial volumes of *Histoire littéraire du sentiment religieux.* And although Bremond would not live long enough to revisit the quarrel over Quietism in the *Histoire* itself, the presence of Fénelon can be detected throughout. Goichot's attentive reading of its volumes discovers evidence "that the rehabilitation of Fénelon must be at one and the same time [its] purpose and goal."[23] When Bremond published *La querelle du Pur Amour au temps de Louis XIII* in 1932, he explicitly stated there that, although not itself the subject of the period under review, "the final duel between Bossuet and Fénelon" is "never lost from view here," nor is Fénelon himself, not "for a single instant."[24] Already, then, over 1909 to1913 Bremond concentrates his attention on the beginning and the end: Jeanne de Chantal on the one hand, Fénelon and Madame Guyon on the other.

But on Fénelon at the expense of Guyon. Bremond seems to have connected with the archbishop in an interior way, given their common

22. Alastair Guinan, "Portrait of a Devout Humanist: M. l'Abbé Henri Brémond," *Harvard Theological Review* 47 (1954): 15–53, at 31.

23. Goichot, "Bremond and Madame Guyon," 173. Albert Cherel, in *Fénelon ou la religion du pur amour* (Paris: Denoël et Steele, 1934), concurs.

24. Henri Bremond, *La querelle du Pur Amour au temps de Louis XIII* (Paris: Bloud et Gay, 1932), 5, 127.

experience of spiritual aridity. As he wrote in the *Apologie:* "When one is reduced to living by pure faith, that is, when it is necessary that one resign oneself to not feeling within oneself God's presence and action, one searches instinctively about oneself for some privileged soul in whom this action and presence is reflected."[25] As Fénelon in relation to Guyon, so Bremond in relation to the succession of mystics he studied in the pages of the *Histoire.*

One final parallel suggests itself: just as taking up Fénelon's cause against Bossuet at the time of the original controversy could have unpleasant consequences for its partisan, so taking up that cause in the early twentieth century could carry its price. André Blanchet has made a strong case that the Indexing of *Sainte Chantal* in May of 1913 proceeded from the book's departure from the traditional conventions of hagiography in depicting the saint's relationship with François de Sales, and was also possibly retribution for Bremond's involvement in L'Affaire Tyrrell. But Blanchet acknowledges as a further motive reprisal for Bremond's contesting the canonical portrait of Bossuet in the *Apologie pour Fénelon,* thereby inciting the ire of ecclesiastical, academic, and political traditionalists.[26]

In short, the *Apologie* is not a marginal work in Bremond's corpus, but stands at the intersection of interests that remain important to him and of forces opposing him along a number of fronts. We may now turn to the work itself.

Bremond's *Apologie*

At its outset, Bremond's *Apologie* resembled a play more than a history, and its author a storyteller more than a serious historian.[27] He begins

25. Bremond, *Apologie,* 42–43. See Goichot, "Bremond et Madame Guyon," 178–79.

26. André Blanchet, *Histoire d'une mise à l'Index: la "Sainte Chantal" de l'Abbé Bremond* (Paris: Aubier-Montaigne, 1967), 50. Guinan shares this assessment of the *Apologie's* share in the factors that contributed to the book's censure (31).

27. Bremond's *Apologie* attracted the notice of a reviewer who found its appearance "too disconcerting" and doubted "that M. Bremond always takes his subject seriously, or, at least, his reader." Notice on Albert Delplanque, *Fénelon et ses amis* in *Études* 125 (1910): 869–70, at 870. As a counterpoint François Varillon states that in the "Pro Fenelone" articles and in the

like a dramatist assembling a large cast of characters and then sorting them out for his audience into those ranged against Fénelon, those who supported him (a shorter list) and other representatives of both camps who were active in Rome. The history of the controversy is then outlined as a drama in five acts.

Driving the action of Bremond's *Apologie* was a conspiracy that continually enflamed the controversy between Bossuet and Fénelon. In Bremond's estimation,

> As with nearly all dramas, this one is directed from offstage. An obscure force tirelessly and unremittingly works to set the two protagonists at odds, who initially asked only to come to an agreement. One—or several—invisible persons manage the play, stymie all attempts at conciliation, tear up the peace treaties and infuse the combatants with ever renewed ardor.[28]

Based on the state of the available documentation, Bremond acknowledged that the identities of the conspirators must remain in part conjectural. However, he hopes that as yet unpublished sources will one day yield hard evidence. Even in the absence of such evidence, Bremond invoked the conspiracy to address a difficulty that has puzzled more than one commentator on this phase of Quietism—given the specialist nature of the substantive issues, how to account for the extent of the interest and involvement in the controversy, its escalation and enduring effects?

As laid out by Bremond, the conspiracy has a political dimension centered on court intrigue grafted onto an anterior coalition ranged against Madame Guyon, both of those set within a broader conflict between Port-Royal and the Jesuits and forming one of the latter's phases. That court intrigue was significant factor in the controversy is suggested by several of its contemporaries, indeed by Fénelon himself, and is accorded a pivotal role in this reconstruction.[29] The influence at court

Apologie, Bremond "pleaded a case considered lost, reopened the dossier of an affair filed away definitively. He did so with an enthusiasm and a spirit that concealed from the view of many the seriousness of his project and the solidity of his information." François Varillon, *Fénelon et le pur amour* (Paris: Éditions de Seuil, 1957), 21.

28. Bremond, *Apologie*, 46–47.

29. Ibid., 47–48.

of a small group which included Fénelon had aroused jealousy, disaffection with the moral tenor of their influence, and in some cases a desire to supplant them. Seeing that a frontal attack was likely to be ineffective, opponents had recourse to more covert means. Here "conspiracy" takes on the aspect of a coalescence of interests, fears, or even a shared taste for slander rather than the dimensions of an organized cabal with clandestine meetings in cellars, though Bremond is able to detect a degree of direction as well.[30]

Hostility to Madame Guyon reinforced the opposition to Fénelon's influence at court. Even before she met Fénelon in 1688, Madame Guyon had experienced a checkered career. While her virtue and sincerity were attested by several prelates, her lack of tact and moderation in proclaiming her spiritual teaching rendered her a less than welcome presence in their dioceses. Although her book on prayer, the *Moyen court et très facile de faire oraison,* gained the approval of ecclesiastical censors and an audience among the devout, she was detained and interrogated by order of the Archbishop of Paris for several months just prior to her initial meeting with Fénelon.

Bremond does not feel compelled to rehearse these events at any length, instead drawing attention to Guyon's autobiography and limiting himself to several incidents that lead him to identify a second plot directed at her expressly. For instance, he questions the driving motives behind Archbishop Harlay's detention of Guyon; given that ecclesiastic's worldly lifestyle an interest in sound doctrine or in spiritual practice are unlikely possibilities. Moreover, in her autobiography Guyon herself mentions repeated slanders regarding her conduct with her confessor, Père La Combe, forged documents designed to discredit her with the king, and prolonged persecutions at the instigation of persons unnamed but who are identified with the Jansenist party. In this evidence of sustained and orchestrated activity, Bremond finds warrant for a second conspiracy directed against Guyon.

Bremond also identifies a third conspiracy, "more vast" and "more imposing" than the ones directed against Fénelon or Madame Guyon.[31]

30. Ibid., 49–50.
31. Ibid., 54–55.

He admits that this third conspiracy remains the most conjectural of the three, but insists that "it rests on certitudes."[32] That the Jesuits took up Fénelon's cause after the publication of the *Maximes des Saints* both at Versailles and at Rome is a matter of record. On record too is their energetic denunciation, but a few years earlier, of the Quietist errors of Miguel de Molinos. Bremond finds it hardly credible that, following upon the condemnation of Molinos by the Holy See, the Jesuits would suddenly be converted to a new Quietism associated with Fénelon and Madame Guyon. And, while sound doctrine mattered to the Jesuits, he argues that it was not their sole concern. Behind Bossuet "were concealed other combatants whom the Jesuits had encountered on other ground and behind other masks, in a word Port-Royal, which would have been less envenomed against the book and Fénelon's person if, beyond this book and this person, it had not seen the Company itself."[33] The engagement of Bossuet with Fénelon thus emerges as the second phase of an ongoing conflict between Jesuits and Jansenists whose first round had concerned moral laxity and had achieved lasting notoriety with Pascal's *Lettres provinciales*—"two links in the same chain, two stages in the same conspiracy."[34] Bremond also discusses the antiQuietist work of the Jansenist Pierre Nicole, written in close proximity to the *Maximes* and influential on Bossuet.

Against this background, the catalyst for the quarrel over Quietism between Fénelon and Bossuet is not simply the former's *Maximes* nor the latter's *Instruction sur les états de l'oraison* (1697). Nor is it the person of Madame Guyon, despite the fact that in her defense Fénelon refused his approval to Bossuet's book and wrote his own in view of it. The pivotal figure is Madame de Maintenon. It is she who "sets the drama going" and who serves as a nexus for bringing the three conspiracies into a focused unity.[35] In opening their circle to Madame de Maintenon, Fénelon and those associated with him at court gained a powerful ally in their efforts to raise the moral standards of the monarchy and

32. Bremond invites historians who remain unconvinced by his explanation to propose alternatives of their own (55).

33. Bremond, *Apologie*, 56–57.

34. Ibid., 57.

35. Ibid., 67.

the spiritual life of France. But in doing so they exposed their mystical teachings to the political fortunes of their ally. While Madame de Maintenon harbored reservations about the person of Madame Guyon, she warmed, at least initially, to the spirituality of the *Moyen court* and granted its author free access to the convent of Saint-Cyr and its school for the shelter and education of indigent daughters of the nobility—a project maintained by Louis XIV and under the patronage of Madame de Maintenon. Through the indiscretions of her cousin, Madame de Maisonfort, who as superior of Saint-Cyr was if anything more enthusiastic over the mystical language of states of the soul, disinterested love, annihilation, and the trials of the spiritual adept, Guyon's ideas circulated well beyond the audience for which they were intended. Over the year 1692, the indiscriminate reading of Guyon's writings led to a breakdown of discipline at Saint-Cyr and a suspicion of heterodoxy attached itself to their author. She was interdicted from visiting the convent, but the contagious stigma of Quietism had surfaced leaving Madame de Maintenon the problem of how to deal with it. Association with a suspect woman whose confessor languished in prison afforded an opening to her own adversaries.[36]

For Bremond these are the events that afford the occult detractors of Madame Guyon, stiffened in their resolve by her recent growth in influence at court through the support of Madame de Maintenon, a new window of opportunity. Aligned with them were those who, out of jealousy or ambition, found a point of vulnerability in Fénelon's close association with Guyon. Thus, in Bremond's view, Madame de Maintenon's initial strategy was to detach Fénelon from Guyon, for which she enlisted the aid of Bossuet. When that failed, she distanced herself from Fénelon, though without desiring or foreseeing the escalation of the controversy that ensued.[37] From roughly July of 1693 to March of

36. Ibid., 70–71.

37. It should not be inferred that Bremond focused exclusively on the political dimensions of these events. As a spiritual director Fénelon was not swayed by political position or social rank and did not mitigate his severity—when severity was needed—out of deference to Madame de Maintenon's status. This was not the type of direction she was used to receiving. Moreover, she had succeeded in rising to high station in the political arena. The stages of the spiritual life proved more difficult. "Fénelon never harbored any illusions regarding her. . . . [S]he never really

1695, Bremond therefore designated Madame de Maintenon the "principal character of the drama."[38]

By emphasizing the political dimensions of the controversy, Bremond implicitly challenged the accusation that Fénelon acted primarily to satisfy his own ambition. Fénelon's critics simply imputed to him their own aspirations. Bremond also makes it clear that, however bizarre they found aspects of Guyon's behavior, Fénelon and his circle regarded her interior life as valid, validated as it was by the effects of her direction on their own religious experience.[39] Thus it was not a case of his being taken in by a mystical poseur and then being too proud to own up to his susceptibility to deception. Moreover, to anticipate, the defects of Guyon's spiritual instruction that stemmed from the deficiencies of her own expression or its misapplication at the hands of others do not compromise its value, when rightly handled and rightly understood. The same can be said of Fénelon's attempts at a more measured exposition of that instruction.

This framing of the controversy also sets the terms on which Bremond will position and judge the substantive issues that arise between Fénelon and Bossuet. Bremond credits Bossuet with "a power of rapid assimilation and of synthesis truly extraordinary." But such formidable talents did not, could not, compensate a deviation that marked the debate from its outset: "He wanted to triumph too quickly, and satisfy, without further delay, Mme de Maintenon's impatience."[40] He accepted, in other words, her alarm over dangerous errors contained in Guyon's writings and read them from that perspective. Second, by his own admission Bossuet was a relative novice where mystical literature was concerned. As late as 1693 he had still not read the *Traité de l'amour de Dieu* nor any works by John of the Cross—"excellent books, of im-

penetrated this doctrine. . . . In the end she sees that the doctrine is not good for her, which is very true, and she concludes in consequence that the same doctrine is bad for everyone, which is very false." Bremond, *Apologie*, 72, 74.

38. Ibid., 82.

39. Bremond makes no secret of his own allegiances: "The spiritual maternity of Mme Guyon is ridiculed. Ridiculous or not, I prefer it to the dry, domineering, denouncing, and persecuting maternity of Madame de Maintenon." *Apologie*, 79.

40. Ibid., 117.

peccable doctrine and which are to the 'spirituals' what the summa of Saint Thomas is to the theologians."[41] Together, these limitations dictated the nature of Bossuet's response to Fénelon. In Bremond's view:

> Two roads are open to him: one, patient and circuitous: slowly examining the prayer of Mme Guyon and that of Fénelon in light of authorized mystics; the other simple, smooth, rapid: to set the writings of the two suspects in opposition with the essential dogmas of Christianity. Here again, he does not hesitate. He leaves aside the complicated problem of mystical psychology and plunges into dogma that he commands better than any other. Thenceforth his entire effort is directed toward uncovering the multiple heresies, the innumerable absurdities of the *Moyen court,* of the *Torrents* and all the rest. It is the method of his great campaigns against Protestantism. On this ground he excels, in the present case it was not the proper ground.[42]

While Bossuet interprets Madame Guyon's writings in light of doctrine, Fénelon judges them against her prayer. At issue is more than a matter of infelicitous expression or of correcting excesses in her teaching; at issue for him is the basic soundness of the mystical tradition as expressed in modern authors such as François de Sales. For that reason, Fénelon consistently defended Guyon against attack.

The discussions among Bossuet, the Sulpician Louis Tronson, and Louis-Antoine de Noailles—at that time Bishop of Chalôns, that issued in the Articles of Issy, affirmed the legitimacy of the prayer of self-surrender and quiet while at the same time cautioning that the extraordinary ways of prayer were rare and subject to the investigation of the bishops.[43] The first affirmation reflects Fénelon's position, while the second reflects Bossuet's. The examination of Guyon and her writings did not succeed in gaining Madame de Maintenon's objective of detaching Fénelon from the teaching of the *Moyen court,* which he continued to regard as fundamentally sound at its base—if admittedly in need of explanation, correction or even retraction on some points—or from

41. Ibid., 116.

42. Ibid., 117–18.

43. Though he did not attend their deliberations, Fénelon established a virtual presence through his continual submission of quotations from the great mystics, accompanied by his explanations of their teaching.

its author. Nor had the Issy conferences succeeded in truly reconciling the different approaches to mysticism on the parts of Bossuet and Fénelon, or indeed their different evaluations of its nature and extent among Catholics. These differences would soon emerge in a series of published exchanges between the two ecclesiastics, culminating in the examination of the *Maximes* and condemnation of propositions drawn from its pages.

The story of those events has been told by Bremond and others and need not be retrieved here.[44] Instead, taking stock of his judgments on the controversy, it is clear that Bossuet and Fénelon are far from agreement on mysticism. For Bremond, these differences are in part attributable to their experiences of spiritual direction: Fénelon's "so-called Quietism responds to the needs of souls at least as he knows them, just as the so-called antiQuietism of Bossuet responds to his personal experience." Indeed, these may well be "the principal difference between these two minds," a difference that Bremond does not seek to resolve "because it does not imply any disagreement on the truths of the faith."[45]

While declining to resolve their disagreement, Bremond is willing to compare their respective spiritualities with the experiences of spiritual directors with the souls entrusted to their care and with the writings of the most accredited spiritual authors. And here Fénelon carries the day. Making allowances for differences in form, "fundamentally they all speak as Fénelon."[46] Indeed, in some of his own letters of spiritual direction Bossuet sounds more like his adversary in the Quietist controversy than he does like himself.[47]

44. A summary exposition of the series of exchanges between Bossuet and Fénelon in the course of the controversy may be found in Ch. Libouroux, *Controverse entre Bossuet et Fénelon au sujet du quiétisme de Madame Guyon* (Paris: Victor Palmé, 1876), ch. 8.

45. Bremond, *Apologie*, 457–58.

46. Ibid., 464.

47. Further, in the *Apologie* Bremond affirms, in company with the Jesuit, Père de Caussade, "that even in his antiquietist writings, [Bossuet] admitted 'confusedly and in isolated fragments', the doctrine that he finds so injurious and absurd under his rival's pen" (469). In 1931 Bremond republished de Caussade's *Instructions spirituelles en forme de dialogues sur les divers états d'oraison suivant la doctrine de M. Bossuet* [1741], *On Prayer: Spiritual Instructions on the Various States of Prayer According to the Doctrine of Bossuet, Bishop of Meaux* [1931], Eng-

Underlying divergences in spirituality are differences in anthropology. Bremond contrasts "the Christian Hellenism of Fénelon" with the "rigorous Augustinianism of Bossuet."[48] The leading ideas that animate Fénelon's writings on disinterested love are evident in his anti-Jansenist work. Bossuet's supernatural psychology, interestingly, has strong affinities with that of the Jansenist Pierre Nicole, as do his judgments regarding mysticism.[49] Nonetheless, beyond their considerable differences, Bremond concludes, Bossuet and Fénelon agree on fundamentals.[50]

Fénelon beyond Bremond

Commentators generally agree that Bremond played an instrumental role in gaining a more equitable evaluation of Fénelon and a correspondingly more critical perspective on Bossuet. Nonetheless, the very nature of his intentions in the *Apologie pour Fénelon* imposed certain limitations

lish trans. Algar Thorold (Springfield, Ill.: Templegate, 1960)—under the title, *Bossuet, maître d'oraison* (Paris: Bloud & Gay, 1931). Although de Caussade credits Bossuet for enabling him to distinguish between false mysticism and its true form, in Bremond's view the bishop's name and reputation are used as a cover to advocate the legitimacy of mystical prayer. Actually, "the student here is not Caussade but Bossuet" (xii). And in reality there emerge two Bossuets: one who, for one phase of his life, polemicizes against the mystics; the other, who "during nearly all his life, appropriated, spontaneously and joyously, if not the technicalities, at least the spirit of the mystics" (xxxiv). On de Caussade see Michel Olphe-Galliard, *La théologie mystique en France au XVIIIe siècle. Le Père de Caussade* (Paris: Beauchesne, 1984), especially ch. 3 and 6.

48. Bremond, *Apologie,* 467.

49. Ibid., 467–68.

50. "The true battle stakes between Bossuet and Fénelon is not a dogmatic system on which the two antagonists in reality are in agreement, but the value of discourse, the value—magnified by Bossuet, contained by Fénelon—of luminous elevations, perceptible devotion and Christian lyricism, in a word all that 'discourse' covers here, as opposed to aridity, to the silencing, obscure and active reality of disinterested love, that is, of a love that does not speak." Henri Bremond, "Une crise dans la vie intérieure de Bossuet," *Annales de philosophie chrétienne* 15 n.s. (October 1912–March 1913): 258–71, at 271.

In a number of suggestive notes (459–86) Bremond identifies several profound differences between Bossuet's spirituality and that of Fénelon—which stand somewhat in tension with his conclusion that there was basic agreement between them. Cf. Bremond's comments in his *Bossuet,* 3 vols. (Paris: Librairie Plon, 1913), 3: 91, where he provides further specification of this facet of their differences. For broader discussion of Bremond's portrayals of Bossuet, see Henry Hogarth, *Henri Bremond: The Life and Work of a Devout Humanist* (London: SPCK, 1950), 17–25.

on his handling of the Quietist controversy. In this Bremond is not alone. As diagnosed by Gabriel Joppin, the engagement with the two principal protagonists tends to place their doctrine in a secondary role. Not that doctrine is forgotten. But it is engaged insofar as it sheds light on the character of its holders, insofar as it appears possible to discern psychological affinities between the two prelates and their respective doctrinal positions. Disinterested love *(pur amour)* with its generosity, its attractiveness, its air of the exceptional, even of the unrealistic appears to be in harmony with the thoroughly pious and aristocratic nature of Fénelon. More of a realist, Bossuet the theologian and man of tradition resists what appears to be departure from the common teaching.

So, for Joppin, "The major theological problem, which was the soul of the conflict, risked being unduly relegated to second rank, or, more seriously still, being deformed and judged according to personal sympathies and antipathies."[51] Joppin proceeded to give two examples in illustration of this tendency: François-Léon Crouslé, whose *Fénelon et Bossuet, études morales et littéraires,*[52] reflects his open partisanship of Bossuet; and Bremond, "all [of whose] writings were, in their own way, the revision of these proceedings in which Fénelon appeared a victim."[53] To the degree to which Bremond was able to bring both Catholic and secular scholars beyond the image of Fénelon that was dominant in the latter half of the nineteenth century, he may be considered to have opened a way to go beyond himself in reengaging the doctrinal basis of the controversy on its own merits.

It is apparent that at the end of the seventeenth century Quietism took on different meanings, not only to Bossuet and Fénelon, but to others who interested themselves in their controversy. It also took on different meanings in different regions. In Italy and Spain, the relationship between meditation and contemplation became the focal point of

51. Gabriel Joppin, *Fénelon et la mystique du pur amour* (Paris: Gabriel Beauchesne, 1938), 6. Cf. Stéphane Harent, "A propos de Fénelon: La question de l'amour pur," *Études* 127 (1911): 178–96; 349–63; 480–500, at 494; 745–68.

52. L. Crouslé, *Fénelon et Bossuet, études morales et littéraires,* 2 vols. (Paris, Honoré Champion, 1894–1895). Boutié's *Fénelon* contains a running engagement with Crouslé's criticism of Fénelon, posing counterfactuals and challenging Crouslé's reading of the data.

53. Joppin, *Fénelon,* 7.

contention. Disinterested love was secondary.[54] It France it was otherwise. Joppin asks, "What is at the basis of all the religious battles of the seventeenth century, be it attritionism and contritionism, Jansenism and Quietism, if not the question of charity?"[55] In the first half of that century, in France there is visible the multiplication, not only of mystical writings, but of mystics. There is also a detectable evolution, captured in the title of Barbara Diefendorf's study, *From Penitence to Charity,* in which she traces a development from a penitential mysticism characteristic of the early part of the century to an emphasis on a compassionate charity that expressed itself in service, above all to the poor.[56]

Such development represents, however, a shift, not a transition. Though attenuated, the ascetical strain will remain strong in French mystical spirituality. (Bremond is faulted by one critic for not attending sufficiently to its presence in Fénelon's direction and practice.)[57] Fed in the late sixteenth century by the writings of Spanish and Rheno-Flemish mystics, and fueled by the religious fervor of the Fronde, mysticism took on a discernibly French ascetic guise, speaking a language of self-abandonment, self-annihilation [*anéantissement*], death to self, nothingness of the creature, which achieved broad currency throughout the seventeenth century.[58] The numerous editions of the works of Saint Catherine of Genoa over the period attest to the saint's popularity and the resonance of her doctrine of the annihilation of self in view of the transformation in God by pure love—affirmed with a certain boldness of expression.[59] This same language achieves prominence among representatives of the French School, reflected in the writings of Pierre

54. Eulogio Pacho, "Quiétisme" (sections on Spain and Italy), in *Dictionnaire de spiritualité,* vol. 12 col. 2756–2805.

55. Joppin, *Fénelon,* 9.

56. Barbara B. Diefendorf, *From Penitence to Charity: Pious Women and the Catholic Reformation in Paris* (Oxford: Oxford University Press, 2004).

57. Goré, *L'itinéraire de Fénelon,* 20.

58. See Mino Bergamo, *La Science des saints* (Grenoble: Jérôme Millon, 1992), ch. 1.

59. Joppin, *Fénelon,* 11. He titles chapter 6 of part II "The Doctor of Disinterested Love: Saint Catherine of Genoa." Louis Cognet notes that Catherine's life and works arrived in France in 1598, translated by Carthusians. Louis Cognet, *Post-Reformation Spirituality,* trans. P. Hepburne Scott (New York: Hawthorne Books, 1959), 58.

de Bérulle, Charles de Condren and Jean-Jacques Olier.[60] Toward the end of the century, then, "disinterested love" and its surrounding vocabulary would not introduce new terminology, but the terms in which it would be presented would be new.

Even before the Quietist controversy, mysticism had its French critics. If mystical writings imported into France came accompanied by the "odor of sanctity" of a Catherine of Genoa, a Teresa of Avila (canonized in 1622) or John of the Cross (beatified in 1675), or bearing the luster of homegrown holiness as with the works of François de Sales (beatified 1662, canonized 1665), they also carried the taint of heterodoxy: the *Alumbrados* in Spain, later the impact of Molinos in Italy. Thus along with the growth of a mystical spirit one can also trace the rise of an antimystical current. At the time of the Quietist controversy, if Fénelon did not have to invent a mystical language, neither did Bossuet have to ferret out Quietist errors *de novo.*[61]

From correspondence, it is evident that Bossuet followed the Molinos affair, but it had only secondary importance for him given his other preoccupations at the time. By 1691 there are indications that he is taking a more direct interest in the excesses of the mystics, but for him it is still a matter of correcting, of moderating tendencies. The following year brings growing reservations. By the time Bossuet comes to be involved personally in Madame Guyon's case, if he is not steeped in the literature of mysticism, he has had exposure to an antimystical, anti-Quietist countercurrent that renders him suspicious of modern ways of spirituality.[62] From his contact with Guyon there emerge the two prin-

60. Cognet remarks that, "like almost all of his period," Bérulle "was influenced to some extent by St Catherine of Genoa." Ibid., 71. On the French School see Yves Krumenacker, *L'école française de spiritualité* (Paris: Cerf, 1998).

61. In 1687 the Bull *Coelestis Pastor,* published in Latin and in French, condemned Quietist errors, serving as a "vulgate of antiquietism." Jacques Le Brun, "Quiétisme" (section on France), in *Dictionnaire de spiritualité,* 2805–12.

62. See Jacques Le Brun, *La spiritualité de Bossuet* (Paris: Librairie C. Klincksieck, 1972), 457–68. Part of this suspicion directed against mysticism derives from Bossuet's perception of it as "modern." As Michel de Certeau points out, "The term 'new' was pejorative at that time." They were innovators—itself enough to discredit them—and wrote in a language replete with jargon, imprecision, and exaggeration. While these criticisms of the "new mystics" are stated with particular force with Bossuet, he is not alone in his reservations regarding them:

cipal problems, or two poles of a single problematic, that will dominate his conflict with Fénelon: disinterested love and activity vs. passivity.

The mystical language of self-abandonment, death to self, and allied terms form a matrix for understanding disinterested love. Spiritual death does not occur without mortification. But asceticism remains rigorously a means. A desire to derive satisfaction for its successful exercise can paradoxically lead to a more subtle form of self-attachment just as one may become attached to consolations that can accompany prayer, and mistake those for love of God.[63] Hence the experience of aridity, even to the point of feeling abandoned by God, that emerges with advancing stages of prayer. In these respects disinterested love stands in continuity with the spiritual tradition. When joined to an Augustinian anthropology that gives primacy to the will, such love entails radical adherence to the will of God, the replacement of the self-will by the divine will, and the forgetfulness of self, of all that prevents or hinders becoming one with God. Problems emerged in relation to the lengths to which this was to be taken.

A central issue became the extent to which disinterested love could be said to be truly disinterested. Could the highest form of love of God renounce all desire for reward, all fear of punishment? Could such love be purified of *all* self-interest? Bossuet thought not. If Fénelon discerned a radical antinomy between love of God and love of self, Bossuet was equally convinced of the impossibility of their separation. In this view, renouncing all hope of reward would be a deformation of the love of God, not its perfection: true love of God and true love of self include hope as in some way immanent in charity. Bossuet therefore considered the self-annihilation as proposed in the *Maximes* to be unattainable: to acknowledge and affirm God as good in himself necessarily encompassed loving God as good for the self.[64]

"Bossuet was no exception and therefore does not deserve the belligerence directed against him by mysticologists since Henri Bremond. He voiced a commonly held view. . . . [A] hundred and one others repeated the stereotype." Michel de Certeau, *The Mystic Fable*, vol. 1, *The Sixteenth and Seventeenth Centuries*, trans. Michael B. Smith (Chicago: University of Chicago, 1992), 108–9.

63. Henri Gouhier, *Fénelon philosophe* (Paris: J. Vrin, 1977), 96.

64. For further development of the differences between the positions of Bossuet and

Here part of the difficulty lay in the imprecision of Fénelon's expression in the *Maximes,* rectified in his later writings.[65] But another part stems from the relative emphasis that he gives to spiritual purification relative to spiritual transformation. In this respect Madame Guyon may be considered to have been better balanced between spiritual death and spiritual resurrection.

On this point Madame Guyon's thought is more nuanced, for if, with her also, our self is destined to die, its true destiny nevertheless is to come to life in God afterward. This resurrection, to which Madame Guyon willingly pays attention in her writings, remains a blindspot in Fénelon's doctrine, whose spirituality insists nearly uniquely in the "annihilation" of the self. The mystical night which for John of the Cross represents a stage in the ascension toward God, tends to become with him an end in itself. It is understandable that, from such a perspective, he is not inclined to insist on everything which concerns the mystery of Redemption and less still on the virtue of hope, both of which could only too easily subsist as forms of self love.[66]

Bossuet's opposition, then, was based on his judgment that disinterested love had been taken to inordinate lengths with Madame Guyon and with Fénelon. Moreover, its consequences also evoked his resistance. When antinomy between love of God and love of self was transposed onto the terrain of divine and human activity, an intensification of the transforming work of grace diminished human activity. Here again the influence of an Augustinian anthropology may be discerned with its correlative emphasis on the absolute sovereignty of God. The corruption of human nature and its corresponding weakness finds its counterpart in the grandeur of God and reliance on his initiative. In short, "holy indifference" could easily be construed as leading to "holy passivity" in

Fénelon on pure love, see Jean-Lydie Goré, *La notion de l'indifférence chez Fénelon au sujet du quiétisme du Madame Guyon* (Paris: Presses Universitaires de France, 1956), part II.

65. For helpful clarification see Moïse Cagnac, *Fénelon: Études critiques* (Paris: Société française d'imprimerie et de librairie, 1910), 327–30.

66. Henk Hillenaar, "Madame Guyon et Fénelon," in *Madame Guyon,* 145–71, at 166–67. He generalizes the danger lurking in this sort of imbalance: "Perhaps it concerns a tendency or a risk inherent in many mystical movements, Christian and other. Often their spiritual retreat becomes regression, their desire for God desire for death. From the vantage point of those who view them, their preoccupation with death—with negation, refusal—seems to assume too great a prominence in their existence, and not only as a metaphor" (170).

advanced souls—so great becomes the emphasis on God's work in the soul that the active exercise of virtue can become lost to view. Here again part of the difficulty resides in choice of language. Fénelon's referring to indifference as a "state" raised a new point of difficulty for Bossuet for it seemed to preclude individual acts of virtue and reinforced a general sense of passivity in the spiritual life. Although this conclusion was neither Guyon's nor Fénelon's intention, their attempts to communicate a continuing necessity for virtuous acts within an overall context of radical dependence upon God were not successful.[67]

The identification of the passive state and disinterested love served as the keystone of the system by which Fénelon sought to organize and systematize the teaching of the mystics. Their juxtaposition subjected each to a reciprocal influence by the other, which evoked resistance and eventual condemnation. While problems with terminology far from exhaust the controversy, less than surprisingly they are highlighted in more recent scholarly appraisals. Nonetheless, the consciousness that doctrine remains central is apparent. Already in 1910, writing after the appearance of Bremond's *Apologie,* Stéphane Harent took issue with that book's conclusion that the quarrel between the two great churchmen was "for nothing, since in truth the two combatants are in agreement on the fundamentals."[68] Indeed, had not Bremond himself given indications of the profound differences between their respective spiritualities?

Conclusion

If, then, Bremond does not have the final word on the Quietist controversy, he did make a notable contribution to rehabilitating Fénelon, thereby enabling subsequent scholarship to move beyond personalities and concentrate more on the substantive issues with a greater objectivi-

67. See Henri Bourgeois, "Passivité et activité dans le discours et l'expérience de madame Guyon," in *Madame Guyon,* 235–67 and the discussion of "indifference" by Mayumi Murata, "Les réactions de Fénelon d'après la condamnation," in *Fénelon. Mystique et politique (1699–1999),* F.-X. Cuche and J. Le Brun (Paris: Honoré Champion, 2004), 137–46.

68. Harent, "A propos de Fénelon," 767, quoting *Apologie,* 475.

ty than was previously possible. Central to his rehabilitation of Fénelon was his emphasis on the personal and pastoral religious experience of the two partisans. In this emphasis, Bremond was a man of his time who participated in the Modernist revival. The Modernist movement made an issue of the status of religious experience. At best an ancillary to the theological enterprise in the dominant neo-Thomism, with its speculative orientation, experience became integral to the Modernists' rethinking of revelation (e.g., with Alfred Loisy), to their understanding of the practical ramifications of dogma (e.g., with Édouard Le Roy), and to their engagement with spirituality (e.g., George Tyrrell).[69] Indeed, it may be argued that one of the more enduring legacies of Modernism, at least in the shorter term, was its contribution to the rehabilitation of mystical experience. In this regard Bremond's publications played a significant role.[70]

69. T. Howland Sanks, *Authority in the Church: A Study in Changing Paradigms* (Missoula, Mont.: Scholars Press, 1974), 118–19, 143, 158–60.

70. Certainly the Modernist attempts to do justice to the subjective dimension of revelation were judged inadequate, as were its pragmatic formulations of dogma. Loisy's "petits livres rouges" had found their way onto the Index in 1903, as had Le Roy's *Dogme et critique* in 1907. By contrast, a renewed interest in mysticism necessarily entailed a positive engagement with experience.

4 Maurice Blondel

Philosophy, Prayer, and the Mystical

Michael J. Kerlin

Although references to the mystical appear frequently in his writings, Maurice Blondel devoted just one essay, "Le problème de la mystique" (1925), formally to the topic. In the essay, he has three goals: (1) to defend the legitimacy of a philosophical consideration of the mystical; (2) to show the relationship of the mystical, considered as a supernatural condition and activity, to natural human conditions and activities; and (3) to reject various approaches to the mystical that either deny philosophy its role or distort this relationship between nature and grace.[1] We could profitably consider any of these aspects of Blondel's thought. George Worgul, for instance, makes a valuable contribution to our understanding of the second issue in his 1987 article, "Blondel and the Problem of Mysticism," where he connects "Le problème de la mystique" with an earlier work *Le procès de l'intelligence* in order to show the significance of connatural knowledge for understanding the mystical.[2] Here I intend to cover some of the same ground as Worgul, but to do so as part of a somewhat different project, one not within Worgul's scope nor directly envisaged by Blondel himself in "Le problème de la mystique." My objec-

1. Maurice Blondel, "Le problème de la mystique," in *Qu'est-ce que la mystique? Cahiers de la nouvelle Journée* 3 (Paris: Bloud et Gay, 1925), 1–63.

2. George Worgul, "Maurice Blondel and the Problem of Mysticism," *Ephemerides theologiae Lovanienses* 61 (1985): 100–22.

tive is to develop Blondel's thought on philosophy insofar as philosophy is itself a form of prayer, having its fulfillment in the mystical by relating "Le problème de la mystique" to comments on the task of philosophy across his entire career.

"Le Problème de la Mystique"

I need to begin by saying something about the use of "the mystical" [*la mystique*] instead of "mysticism" [*le mysticisme*] in the title. George Worgul not only entitles his article "Blondel and the Problem of Mysticism," but also writes of mysticism throughout the article. Blondel himself gave reason for using "mysticism" and "the mystical" interchangeably, albeit with care, in a 1908 note for André Lalande's *Vocabulaire technique et critique de la Philosophie.*[3] However, in "Le problème de la mystique" Blondel insists on a distinction from the onset. Thus in the first footnote: "I will hardly employ this equivocal term [*mysticisme*] which one abuses; for ordinarily words with *-ism* indicate not facts or realities but abstractions or tendentious, even exclusive, explanations."[4] It becomes clear a little further on that Blondel's concern is not just with abstractions or tendentiousness. Mysticism had come to imply features that Blondel distinguishes from the mystical.

> [B]ecause it evokes thus too easily the image of a sort of mysterious effervescence at the heart of that which Pseudo-Dionysius . . . called . . . "the Great Darkness," many believe themselves to be able indistinctly to combine under this term all that is *pathos* and *Patmos*: smoky ardors of instinct, troubled effusions of sentiment, cloudy sublimities of passion, bad and good romanticism, the ecstasies of the flesh and ravishments of the spirit. There is nothing astonishing thus, if for a number of wise people, suspicion persists, if hostility prevails against these uncontrolled powers that tend to usurp the supreme wisdom.[5]

In this excerpt Blondel criticizes a confused talk of the mystical, but in the next paragraph he makes his own verbal distinction clear. "If ordinar-

3. André Lalande, *Vocabulaire technique et critique de la philosophie* (Paris: Librairie Félix Alcan, 1926), 497–98.

4. Blondel, "Le problème de la mystique," 2–3, n. 1.

5. Ibid., 3–4.

ily illusions are based on faint resemblances, here it is clear for anyone who can see that the dissemblances are profound, the contradictions are real between 'false mysticism' and 'the true and only mystical.'"[6]

Consequently we are not surprised to find that "Le problème de la mystique" is neither about theories of mysticism nor about the human phenomena captured under the label *faux mysticisme.* But what is "la vraie et seule mystique" that Blondel would study? The juxtaposition of *faux mysticisme* and *vraie mystique* in the opening paragraphs would seem to allow for a philosophical consideration of experiences and happenings in many religions and cultures, all qualifying as vraie mystique without any prioritizing of the experiences and happenings within one religious community and without a commitment to a particular theological interpretation of them. Such a consideration would have something of the scope of William James's *Varieties of Religious Experience* or W. T. Stace's *Mysticism and Philosophy.* But that is not the direction Blondel takes: *la vraie et seule mystique* of "Le problème de la mystique" is something specifically Christian with its proper terms of interpretation coming from the Roman Catholic tradition.

Although Blondel gives no definition of *la vraie mystique,* it becomes clear that he understands *la vraie mystique* to be a matter of a contemplative union with God, coming to human beings as a special infused grace beyond anything achievable by human effort and beyond the expectations grounded by any philosophical analysis.[7] Late in the essay Blondel refers to the possibility of a genuine mystical experience outside Christianity, making particular reference to Islam. But this experience "cannot be without the soul of the Church, without real participation in the graces of Christ, which have nothing in common with the exaltation of blind forces."[8] The question then of "Le problème de la mystique" is about the bearing of philosophy on an area of life that Blondel considers formally supernatural according to the common nature-supernature distinction of Roman Catholic theology. He wants to work as a philosopher at the interface of faith and reason, theology, and philosophy.

6. Ibid., 6.

7. Ibid., 19, 26, 42n., 44, and 46.

8. Ibid., 59.

Even a reader who knew nothing of the controversies of the day could recognize from comments made at many junctures in "Le problème de la mystique" that Blondel makes his arguments against real opponents, who are quoted in places even if never identified by name. Some of these opponents had denied the legitimacy of any philosophical approach to the mystical in order to protect philosophy by keeping it in its own domain. Others denied the legitimacy of any philosophical approach to the mystical in order to maintain the transcendence and gratuity of the properly mystical. Blondel's most immediate response to both sets of critics follows Aristotle in the *Metaphysics*: "If it is necessary to philosophize, then philosophize; if it is necessary not to philosophize, it is necessary to philosophize if only to make precise the reasons for not doing so." Blondel adds, "In sum, there are no facts outside of reason, against reason: one can speak of the illogical, not of the alogical."[9]

Blondel also responded at greater length to these two opposing criticisms. He himself had been accused of developing a type of mysticism in the name of philosophy ever since the defense of *L'Action,* his 1893 doctoral dissertation. Although he responded to that charge many times over the years, he doesn't avert to it in "Le problème de la mystique." I shall be saying more about his sense of himself as a philosopher in the sections to follow. To the second line of criticism, that he compromises the supernatural character of *la vraie et seule mystique* both by his philosophical method and by the manner of his analysis, Blondel replies that the critics who bar philosophical analysis run the risk of envisaging the mystical as irrational in the sense of *faux mysticisme* and of making it something accidental, extrinsic, and artificial (the word *postiche* recurs throughout the essay).[10]

"Le problème de la mystique" does more than defend the role of philosophy in the analysis of the mystical. The article also proposes a particular way of connecting infused contemplative union with ordinary experience. The highest level of knowledge involves a type of connaturality, that is, a knowledge in which the knower apprehends reality

9. Ibid., 8.
10. Ibid., 11, 18, and 38.

directly in a way beyond anything conveyed in concepts. This knowing will be cognitive as well as affective, intellectual as well as practical. In the case of the mystical, "the actual conditions of exercising our intelligence prevent all direct perception of spiritual and divine realities." Knowledge about the mystical must remain "a sort of obscure knowledge . . . blind and stumbling yet becoming, as it were, a type of view." It is a knowledge that "permits us constant experience of the Godhead, rendering us *connatural* with God."[11] Blondel's task is to show that this mystical knowledge "actualizes certain potentials, certain very profound and excellent obediential potencies" on the natural level.[12]

If the "true and only mystical" involves a type of connaturality, then it would make sense to find these potentials in ordinary experience.

> I am then going to maintain: that there is normally a real knowledge by connaturality; that it is truly a knowledge; that it has a normal function in the natural order, a value at the same time practical and contemplative, an objective import; that there is a solidarity and a heterogeneity between its role in the natural order and its role, indispensable in effect, in the supernatural order and more yet in the order properly mystical to which it contributes by clearing the path and permitting exact specification.[13]

This "real knowledge by connaturality" will be something aconceptual, not in the sense that it will be apart from abstract knowledge, but that it will not be the same as abstract knowledge. At the same time, it will not be purely affective or purely practical. It will, in the terms stated above, be really cognitive and really intellectual.

Do we have such connatural knowledge? Blondel's approach in the essay is largely a priori, proceeding mainly from a theory of knowing rather than from examples. Knowledge is primarily of the real, of the concrete, and of the universal as the union of concrete realities. Abstractions enable us to clarify what we have already understood in a more primordial way: neither they nor things known through them are the final point of knowing.

> Abstract and discursive science can be in us only a partial extract, an abstract of this concrete thought, which is in original and constant communion

11. Ibid., 28.
12. Ibid., 7.
13. Ibid., 30.

with integral reality. . . .This notional knowledge marks an awakening and a progress of the spirit through a movement toward goals superior to nature, a victory over the mountain in sand of sensations, a means of traversing the infinite dust of facts, yes, assuredly. But it is only the boring of the tunnel permitting passage through the semiobscure to the full and free light of a wisdom which does not live uniquely from facts and from abstractions, from generalities and theory.[14]

Blondel's critics see knowledge as something acquired once and for all "in an immobile and impenetrable block" and as having no rapport with the experiences of life or even with the analyses of reflection. In response, Blondel gives examples of knowledge by connaturality. This knowledge has its own methods, always in development and imperfect, but methods nonetheless. So for example, a musical genius like Mozart is able to hear the whole of a symphony in a sovereign idea, and a mathematician like Descartes comes to simple intuitions embracing a whole chain of demonstrations as the result of prolonged reviews of the whole and entirely free enumerations of the parts.[15]

Blondel's fullest treatment of the knowledge by connaturality was in his 1921, "Le procès de l'intelligence." Here too he wrote in the context of an ongoing controversy, this time responding to the priority given to intelligence over intuition by Charles Maurras and other writers of *L'Action française*. Blondel's long essay was the lead piece in a book edited by his friend Paul Archambault. In the essay, he takes Archambault's lead in seeing intelligence as the faculty, or the act, of understanding an idea or a thing by "establishing the relations that link them to other ideas or other things, relations that also link the diverse elements of both ideas and things themselves."[16] Blondel argues that intelligence cannot be solely or even primarily a matter of forming concepts and reasoning abstractly. Although he defends the realism of abstract intelligence (against Bergson, for example), he maintains that this realism depends on another type of intelligence, variously called intuition in contrast

14. Ibid.

15. Ibid., 32–33.

16. Maurice Blondel, "Le procés de l'intelligence," in *Le procés de l'intelligence,* Paul Archambault (Paris: Bloud et Gay, 1922), 5–6. The essay first appeared in an edition of *La Nouvelle Journée* 19 (June 1921; July 1921; and August–September 1921).

to discourse, real knowledge in contrast to notional knowledge (John Henry Newman), the spirit of finesse in contrast to the spirit of geometry (Blaise Pascal), and the knowledge by connaturality, or affinity, as against the knowledge by notions (Thomas Aquinas).[17] The two forms of intelligence or knowledge are, in fact, inseparable, having their roots in action and their fulfillment in a union beyond human possibilities.

Blondel continued to reflect on the distinction between, and the relationship of, these two forms of intelligence over the next decade. Clearly, "Le problème de la mystique" draws on the ideas of this earlier essay, a connection that Worgul makes admirably in the article noted in the opening paragraph. Blondel would return to them in the two-volume *La Pensée* of 1934, where he distinguishes between thought-thought and thought-thinking [*la pensée pensée* and *la pensée pensante*] and also between the noetic and pneumatic dimensions of thought. Both distinctions stress the dynamic character of *la pensée pensante* and the pneumatic on the one hand and the relatively static character of *la pensée pensée* and the noetic on the other. But he continued to insist on the realism and importance of the latter.

In the final paragraphs of "Le problème de la mystique," Blondel returns to the relationship of reason and philosophy [*la pensée pensée*] to the mystical [*la pensée pensante*]. It is not only that philosophy has for its realm all of human life and that it serves to locate the mystical itself with this life. The mystical has an essential relationship to the work of philosophy. The mystical may be beyond philosophical possibilities, and the mystic may have no essential need of philosophy, but the mystical is what the philosopher has been pursuing without being able to achieve it on his or her own. Thus Blondel closes the essay with this passage:

> the philosopher, who is not able of himself to discover it, to procure it, to experience it, does he not find it in himself nonetheless to ratify, to admire the perfection of spirit [of the mystical] according to the most essential idea, the most concrete possible that the spirit can have? And ought we not to conclude that in truth, according to the doctrine of St. John of the Cross, the mystic is the most reasonable of men?[18]

17. Blondel, "Le problème de la mystique," 249–69.
18. Ibid., 62–63.

For the remainder of this essay, I would like to develop this connection between philosophy and the mystical and in the process to explore Blondel's suggestive remarks in *L'Action* of 1893 and in *La Pensée* about philosophy and prayer. First I turn to his most powerful consideration of the nature of philosophy, the 1906 articles on "Le point de départ de la recherche philosophique."

"Le point de départ de la recherche philosophique"

"Le point de départ" appeared in the *Annales de philosophie chrétienne* over two issues: January and June 1906. Blondel begins the first article with a question:

> Where does philosophy begin? Is it from one's earliest reflection on the facts of the senses or of knowledge, from one's earliest criticism of the immediate clues of consciousness and the spontaneous hypotheses of reason? Or does it amount to a technical discipline to which access is denied, unless paid for by a precise method, starting from a clearly demarcated line so as to adopt a clearly defined standpoint, from where it can deal with the whole collection of questions it raises?[19]

The history of philosophy suggests that we might justifiably take either direction, but the direction we take will largely determine how we understand the enterprise. Will philosophy be mainly a less formal dimension of life or will it be science? Will it be popular or technical? Or will it be both, as Blondel clearly thinks? His answer is that "philosophical knowledge is specifically distinct from any other . . . that it has a formal character, which sharply determines the beginning of its inquiry and the task it has to fulfill." Thus it has "technical demands" that must be taken into account. But ultimately philosophy has to "fit itself into the common effort of humanity to create a work of life at the same time as one of science."[20] To understand the relationship between these two di-

19. Maurice Blondel, "Le point de départ de la recherche philosophique," *Annales de philosophie chrétienne* 151 (January 1906): 36. See Fiacre Long's English translation, "The Starting Point of Philosophical Research," in *The Idealist Illusion and Other Essays* (Dordrecht: Kluwer Academic, 2000), 115. All citations are from Long's translation.

20. Blondel, "The Starting Point," 115–16.

mensions of philosophy is to understand something more fundamental, the two basic types of knowledge in general, direct knowledge in action and the reflection on this action.

To convey what he means by these two types of knowledge, Blondel proposes that we consider his activity at the very moment of writing. Writing an essay like "Le point de depart" involves many past experiences, themselves the fruit of many previous ideas and projects. But at the moment of writing the writer is wholly given over to the activity of writing. He knows what he is doing: he knows what he is trying to accomplish and he knows how to accomplish it without dwelling on the causes or elements of the activity. Sometimes though, he changes his focus to think about these causes and elements as Blondel has done at some stage of writing "Le point de départ." Now he no longer engages in writing in any ordinary sense. He is studying writing in abstraction "from the precise conditions and the true ends to which this action should be directed." Studying writing has the advantage not only of helping us to comprehend the process of writing, but also of enabling us to reorient ourselves so that we might write differently and perhaps even better. Nonetheless, after he has studied writing and after he has absorbed the results of his study, he must return to writing itself with all the directness that characterized it before he broke away from it for his formal study. Although *réflexion* would suggest itself easily as the right term for formal study, there is no such ready term for the elementary, unselfconscious activity out of which it comes and to which it will at some stage revert. What term shall we use? To make a rhyme on réflection and to stress the always future oriented character of direct knowledge, Blondel proposes the term *prospection*. This distinction and terminology, although never so central as here, would remain part of his thought and vocabulary throughout his work.

The large middle part of "Le point de départ" for January 1906 focuses on the ways in which philosophers have distorted their work by overvaluing one or the other type of knowing in both their ways of philosophizing and in their ways of explaining what they have been doing. Although the most frequent mistake is to exaggerate the reflective character of philosophy, the remedy is not to downplay reflection. It may be an artifice, but it is "a natural and even indispensable artifice." Reflection must be seen as an essential moment in life, in the movement forward toward the goal of action, toward destiny.

Blondel then returns to the consideration of the activity he is engaged in at this moment, that of writing.

Thus, at first sight, the existence of this page which blackens under my pen is in some way linked to the plan I follow in composing these pages, a plan which is itself subordinated to the conception I have of life and of the effort I am making to resolve the problem of my destiny. Yet it is true, even if its truth is sketchy and superficial; for if I think of the invention or the fabrication of paper, if I ask myself why after so many others I learned to write, why I bought these reams of paper, why I chose the subject of this article, is it not the case that everywhere from the nearest to the farthest of my actual intentions, I see two immense series of intertwined, stimulating "prospections" and inventive "reflections"? To rely on one of these series alone in philosophical research is to want to weave a cloth without texture, using thread pointing in one direction only.[21]

We might think that the task of philosophy is to define this relation between prospection and reflection but even this would be itself a false move since it would suppose that they could be separated and then rejoined. In fact, prospection and reflection are inseparable, although distinguishable, from one another. The point of the second article is to consider prospection and reflection in such a way as not to set them up as separate from each other.

Having argued in the first article that "knowledge in act always operates simultaneously through fragmentary reflections and total prospection,"[22] Blondel tries in the second to show that these two inseparable and irreducible aspects of knowledge are no less complementary in philosophy. To make his point, Blondel outlines two challenges and two harmonics of reflection and prospection. The challenge from the standpoint of reflection is to recognize that philosophy cannot begin with "independent problems regarding distinct objects as if they were separately resolvable." On the contrary, it subordinates all of the partial

21. Ibid., 127.
22. Ibid., 129.

perspectives to "the single inevitable problem raised in us by the relations between awareness and action." That is, philosophy sets "its task to clarify the integral synthesis of prospection."[23] The challenge from the standpoint of prospection is to understand and practice "the duty of spelling out, letter by letter, the book of life written in us, of separating its governing ideas, of reaching, of assimilating its composite realities, of foreseeing and preparing their unfolding." If it meets the challenge, philosophy will have "reintegrated into itself all the fragmentary achievements of reflection."[24] It is important to note that philosophy must renounce any premature moral or religious satisfaction. Rather it must proceed "methodically and progressively *singillatim et per gradus debitos"* through the whole inventory of experience and against all doubts that confront it.

Blondel's first harmonic is that, "before any research, before any affirmation about the reality of our being and the reality of the objects that we think, we must first realize what we are really conscious of being and of what we actually think."[25] Thought and its objects, he continues, form "a string of states which are never isolated, unless by abstraction." The result is that the question of "what is" leads us by a type of necessity from one element in the string to another, to "more and more concrete knowledge," thus making "explicit the implicit contents of perception."

The second harmonic is that there is no end to the process of filling in and drawing out, "that reflection never exhausts prospection or exhausts itself, that, neither in us nor outside us . . . can one reach atoms of consciousness or substance by a distinct and irreducible speculative path."[26] Of greatest importance is not this or that moment of knowledge, this or that atom of reality, but the law of development, the overall orientation of thought in its encounter with its world. Philosophy must integrate "everything which manifests the truths of consciousness and science" into life. The consequence will be a reconsideration of the very notion of truth: "Substituted in place of the abstract and chimerical *adaequatio speculativa rei et intellectus* is the methodological research

23. Ibid., 130.

24. Ibid.

25. Ibid., 132.

26. Ibid., 133.

of the *adaequatio realis mentis et vitae.*"[27] Some pages later, Blondel remarks that we shall achieve the *adaequatio realis* only by "an appeal to action and by harvesting action's response."[28] This reconsideration of the notion of truth was to lead to decades of controversy with scholastic philosophers and theologians like Joseph de Tonquédec and Reginald Garrigou-Lagrange.[29]

In the final paragraph, Blondel gathers the thoughts of the essay. Philosophy "imposes technical discipline on itself only in order to respect the same complexities of life, to remain faithful to popular instinct that is always against the knowledge which is not convertible to action."[30] But it will also uphold the importance of abstract thought inasmuch as it signals the elements of experience and of reality and leads us to affirm the connectedness and open-endedness of thinking, doing, and being. We have then a definition of philosophy and an answer to the question about "the starting point of philosophy."

To the initial question it is therefore valid to reply that philosophy is the integration, special and technical in its form, universal and popular in its subject matter, of the ordered efforts of human life to produce our being by producing being and beings within us, that is to say, by knowing them, by adapting ourselves to them, by assimilating them into ourselves.[31]

Taken in these terms, philosophy is an unceasing and necessarily cooperative endeavor requiring the whole of life and all of our lives. And so we might interpret the saying that "philosophy is the apprenticeship of death" as meaning that "it is the anticipation of true life which for us is indivisibly knowledge and action."[32]

27. Ibid., 135.

28. Ibid., 142.

29. Long translates *chimérique* in the section quoted above as nebulous. I have departed from his translation here by using *chimerical.* For a survey of Blondel's disputes on the problem of truth, see my "Blondel and Pragmatism: Truth as the Real Adequation of Mind and Life," in *Papers of the Nineteenth Century Theology Group at the Twentieth Annual Meeting of the American Academy of Religion,* ed. Andrew J. Burgess, David D. Schultenover, Daniel W. Hardy, and Theodore Vial, 90–108; and Francesco Bertoldi, "Il dibattio sulla verità tra Blondel e Garrigou-Lagrange," *Sapienza* 43 (1990): 293–310.

30. Blondel, "The Starting Point," 143.

31. Ibid., 144.

32. Ibid.

Philosophy, Prayer, and the Mystical

The discussion of philosophy in "Le point de départ" proceeds at a high level of abstraction, but we know that Blondel is writing in the essay in part about himself as a philosopher and about philosophy as he would practice it. He is, in fact, writing about his personal vocation and about the vocational ideal of philosophy. However, we can see his sense of personal vocation best in "Mémoire envoyée à Monsieur R. Prêtre de Saint-Sulpice" of September 9, 1893, written a little more than three months after his defense of *L'Action.* The memoir was published in 1961 as an addendum to *Carnets intimes (1883–1894),* selections from his personal notebooks from the years leading up to and just beyond *L'Action.* Blondel describes how the idea of the priesthood as a calling had been with him from childhood but how he had also come increasingly to see himself as called to the work of philosophy, not just as a type of study that gave him satisfaction, but as an apostolate among "misled souls or sincere unbelievers of which my dream from adolescence had been to dissipate their prejudices in speaking their own language."[33] In the midst of all his hesitations he had come to see a clear and complete design.

> I wish to act, in the name of reason even and in the supernatural interest of souls, on the thinkers who reflect and who want to govern themselves by ideas. My ambition is to show that, fully consequent to his resolve of independence, man comes to submit himself to God, that the supreme effort of his nature is to avow the need he has to surpass it, and that his own will prevents him from arriving at his true will.[34]

He finally chooses the life of philosopher as more suitable to his gifts and not unrelated to the ends of the priesthood that had drawn him so powerfully. He would, in pursuit of his vocation, "keep with regard to himself and with regard to others the restlessness of the seeker under the serenity of the believer." Obtaining an appropriate university assignment was not to be easy. The responsible government education official initially recommended denying him such a post on the ground

33. Maurice Blondel, *Carnets intimes (1883–1894)* (Paris: Éditions du Cerf, 1961), 546.
34. Ibid., 550.

that his Christian commitments and philosophical orientations were incompatible with university teaching. Only the intervention of Raymond Poincaré, the minister of education and a family connection of Émile Boutroux, the principal reader of *L'Action,* gained him a professorship at Aix-en-Provence, a position he would hold for the rest of his active career.

Carnets intimes tells us much about Blondel's thought on philosophy itself. On January 24, 1887, he writes, "Philosophy ought to be the sanctity of reason. One is not competent at it because one is intelligent or meditative. It is necessary to be a man, to be a Christian, to be a saint: it is the necessary experience."[35] However, nothing in the notebooks suggests that only Christians, only saints can be philosophers. Rather the explorations of philosophers have their beginning answers in Christianity, in the life of the saints. So he can say in an 1889 entry that "all complete truth is Catholic. Every Catholic has in himself the complete truth. But there are difficulties to explain, to be poured out, to be given to oneself and to others."[36] Working out those difficulties for oneself and for others involves following freely all the false paths of "liberated thought." It means not thinking with those who think as he does, but with those who think against him, a demand that is not purely strategic, but an issue of the very nature of philosophy.[37] It is a rational enterprise that involves confronting every doubt, every intellectual problem, and not being satisfied with any preliminary, unearned satisfaction. Generally in these notebooks we have the sense that the doubt at issue is methodological and not real, but one entry, a year after the defense of his dissertation, leads us to think there is something more at stake for Blondel. "You leave me the vivid and painful sentiment of the obscurity of your ways, of the difficulty of your faith, and, if I dare say, the uncertainty of your existence and revelation. Blessed be you in that uncertainty."[38] But we should leave the intimate elements of *Carnets intimes* aside for a consideration of *L'Action,* the dissertation that was to remain Blondel's most creative and influential achievement, whatever his own judgment in later years.

35. Ibid., 104.
36. Ibid., 210.
37. Ibid., 518.
38. Ibid., 519.

The opening paragraph of *L'Action* gives the tenor of the whole book. Does human life *really* make sense, and does man have a destiny? I act, but without even knowing what action is, without having wished to live, without knowing exactly who I am or even if I am. This appearance of being which flutters about within me, these light and evanescent actions of a shadow, bear in them, I am told, an eternally weighty responsibility, and that, even at the price of blood, I cannot buy nothingness because for me it is no longer. Supposedly, then, I am condemned to life, condemned to death, condemned to eternity! Why and by what right, if I did not know it and did not will it?[39]

Through 446 pages of the English translation, with very few citations and without bibliography, Blondel attempts his personal "essay on a critique of life and a science of practice." He tries to understand what goes on in action and to draw from it a philosophically grounded answer to the questions of the first sentence quoted just above. Starting with the most minimal sense of action, he moves alternatively from the analysis of action to the discussion of the meaning of life. He shows the ways in which we move forward in semi-light by acts of natural faith through wider and wider circles of social involvement to form ourselves and our world. When we make any of these circles a final stopping point, we find ourselves pushed forward by the necessary logic of our situation and our analysis. It is a movement that can logically stop only with the alternative of affirming the possibility of "one thing necessary" beyond all human creations, imaginings, and conceptions. Throughout the book, he insists on taking up the challenges of the nihilist, the dilettante, the positivist, the naturalist, the ethicist, and the deist before he allows himself to move on.

What do we learn about philosophy from *L'Action*? Certainly that a philosophical dissertation is not to be merely an exercise for launching a career—however much its author may have hoped for such a career from it. This dissertation would do no less than answer the riddle of life and action. It would also be a piece of rigorous reasoning: the author

39. Maurice Blondel, *L'Action (1893): Essai d'une critique de la vie et d'une science de la pratique* (Paris: Presses Universitaires de France, 1950), vii. See Oliva Blanchette's translation in *Action (1893): Essay on a Critique of Life and a Science of Practice* (Notre Dame: University of Notre Dame Press, 1984), 3. All citations are from Blanchette's translation.

would take on all comers and would allow himself no easy victories. There is audacity—even a bit of hubris—in the way Blondel takes on adversaries, almost always without name, in the text, and as he would do face to face in the defense. Peter Henrici has fruitfully compared the dialectical method of *L'Action* with that of the *Phenomenology of Spirit*: Blondel and Hegel both step as far back from their goal as possible and use resistance as a means of moving forward.[40] Blondel himself is more conscious of Descartes's *Meditations on First Philosophy* as a model.

Like Descartes, who had feigned new reasons for doubting, we had to make some strange moral attitudes enter into the domain of philosophical doctrines, and to start from further back in order to go further forward than others had gone, from the frame of mind of the aesthete to the devotion of the Grey Nun. But the Methodical Doubt was the singular disposition of a single mind; we have to accept all the diversity of human consciousness and to make even those who feign not to set out at all to go forward. From the Methodical Doubt one emerged as from a fiction; we have to remain in action as in reality. Thus, what was only the problem of the understanding, becomes the problem of the will; it is no longer only the Cartesian question, but the Kantian question which we had to resolve anew by defining the relation of knowing, doing and being.[41]

In *L'Action,* as in "Le problème de la mystique," philosophy poses questions it cannot answer and solutions it cannot verify. The answer and the verification can come only in action, actually in the affirmation of and surrender to "the one thing necessary" in literal practice.

It is for philosophy to show the necessity of posing the alternative: "Is it or is it not?" But philosophy can go no further, nor can it say, in its own name alone, whether it be or not. But if it is permitted to add one word, only one, which goes beyond the domain of human science and the competence of philosophy, the only word able, in the face of Christianity, to express that part of certitude, the best part, which cannot be communicated because it arises only from the intimacy of totally personal action, one word which would itself be an action, it must be said: "It is."[42]

40. Peter Henrici, *Hegel und Blondel* (Pullach: Verlag Berchmanskolleg, 1958).
41. Blondel, *Action,* 444.
42. Ibid., 446.

My sense is that, if philosophy is to be the sanctity of reason, a designation Blondel makes here as in *Carnets intimes,* it is both because it leads to "It is," and also because it assumes all the demands of reason.[43]

The published version of *L'Action* includes a chapter entitled "The Bond of Knowledge and Action in Being," a chapter missing from the version presented to the examining committee. If the committee had seen the chapter, the members might have given Blondel even more trouble than they did. Certainly, it was to prove the most controversial part of *L'Action,* exposing its author to accusations of both fideism and idealism. Blondel maintains in this last chapter before the conclusion that everything preceding in *L'Action* is at the phenomenal level and that only the final decision before the "one thing necessary" confers existential status on the elements of the chain taken singly or collectively. Blondel was to defend himself and the argument against his opponents, most notably in his response to M.-Bénoit Schwalm, "L'illusion idéaliste," and he would omit the chapter in the second volume of the 1936–1937 *L'Action,* where he presents the greater part of the dissertation without revision.[44] We might then bypass the additional chapter here, but it is in fact important for Blondel's whole project and for the present chapter.

I take it, with Henri Bouillard, that the main point of Blondel's chapter is not epistemological but metaphysical. Blondel wants to establish a "metaphysics of the second power," an account where

> appearances, themselves, duration, all the inconsistent forms of individual life, far from being abolished, participate in the absolute truth of the divine knowledge of the Mediator. . . . Called to see all things in the unity of the divine plan, through the eyes of the Mediator, called to see himself in the permanent act of liberality and to love himself in loving the perpetual charity from which he has his being, he is this very act of his author, and he produces it in himself as it is in him.[45]

43. Ibid., 404.

44. M.-Bénoit Schwalm, "Les illusions de l'idéalisme et leurs dangers pour la foi," *Revue Thomiste* 4 (September 1896): 413–14; Maurice Blondel, "L'illusion idéaliste," *Revue de Métaphysique et de Morale* 6 (November 1898): 726–45; Maurice Blondel, *L'Action I–II* (Paris: Presses Universitaires de France, 1947); and Henri Bouillard, *Blondel and Christianity,* trans. James M. Somerville (Washington: Corpus Books, 1969), 104.

45. Blondel, *Action,* 423.

If the concluding "it is" has this metaphysical import, then the infused contemplative union, the true and only mystique of "Le problème de la mystique," will be the earthly fulfillment of the philosophical quest for the union of knowledge, action, and being. It will be a human fulfillment beyond all powers of human intelligence and will.

The position of the preceding paragraphs is consistent with all of Blondel's work from the Latin thesis, *De Vinculo Substantiali et de Substantia Composita apud Leibnitium,* presented prior to *L'Action* at the Sorbonne, to the final writings of the tetralogy. Here I want to invoke just one more text, *La Pensée* of 1934, the initial work of the tetralogy. Blondel devotes a good part of the second volume to a theory of philosophy. Thought, the act of unifying diversity in life, takes two human forms, the pneumatic, that is, the act of thought by which we thrust forward toward goals that we cannot foresee, and the noetic, that is, the act of thought by which we congeal the discoveries of the moment in concepts, principles, theories. Consistent with "Le point de départ," Blondel makes philosophy the bringing together of these two forms of thought. More than an academic discipline, more than an intellectual exercise, it is an act of prayer.

It is not only the man who lives in all philosophy, it is philosophy itself that is and will be always naturally, normally, a figure at prayer [*une orante*]. And this seventh part of our study has been in sum, under the pressure of a consented dialectic as much as an imperative, the exposé of the philosophical prayer, that which, to usurp a term from another provenance, one might call the baptism of desire, of sincerity and of courage. There is, in the thought already alive in us, more than philosophical science is able to exhaust and to systematize; it is then philosophical to recognize and to inscribe on our intellectual maps that terra that we have not the right to name incognita since the view is certain and, in the night even, it is near to us, it is already in us.[46]

And for what do we pray? What would answer our prayers? A few pages earlier Blondel had written about the mystical.

[T]he depth of our intelligence implies always a state which merits the name of "mystical," which, because of its being known indistinctly and because of

46. Maurice Blondel, *La Pensée II: Les Responsibilités de la Pensée et la Possibilité de son Achèvement* (Paris: Presses Universitaires de France, 1954), 270.

the access that it provides, touches where the divine grasps. [It implies] that this word that people so often abuse would not allow us to miss the reasonable and even rationally justified character of a knowledge which, though it may seem nocturnal, is no less an extension of thought all the way to its subterranean source from which overflows its inexhaustible tide. Mystical knowledge, these two words that one accuses sometimes of being incompatible, ought on the contrary to mark a superior degree of truth, of certitude and of propulsive force.[47]

The sentences that follow repeat almost verbatim material from the final pages of "Le problème de la mystique," referring approvingly to Charles Delbos on the superior realism of the true mystic and John of the Cross on his reasonableness. We have come full circle while, I would hope, having enlarged the circle.

Concluding Reflections

Although I have had the commonsense philosopher's skepticism about mystical experiences, about experiences transcending the realm of ordinary life, a commonsense philosopher skeptical about mysticism can still, by my lights, have a concern about spirituality, even prayer. As I re-read "Le problème de la mystique" and the other literature discussed here, I realized that for Blondel the problem of the mystical is, in fact, part of the problem of philosophy. Or, better, that a properly oriented spirituality of philosophy will, on his terms, mean an openness not just to faith, but also to the "true and only mystical" of the essay. In the 1893 *L'Action,* philosophy is prayer from beginning to end, although the prayer becomes increasingly richer, deeper, and broader. Moreover, the mystical is the highest level of prayer and the answer to philosophical questions arising from the imperative of and to action. Anyone who shares, or has shared, Blondel's passion for philosophy and his faith as a Roman Catholic, and perhaps those who do not share them, can appreciate the coherence, indeed the beauty, of this way of bringing philosophy to completion in the fullness of life. But there remain problems in the approach.

47. Ibid., 266.

One set of problems centers on philosophy, an activity understood almost universally as a matter of discourse, embracing questions formulated through discourse and of answers given through discourse. Blondel himself is surely a writer given to long, intricate, and fairly technical discourses. Doesn't then the talk about action, about prayer, about the mystical, make the discourse secondary to something nondiscursive at the beginning (action) and the end (the mystical) with the whole process at heart something nondiscursive (prayer)? Perhaps, though, Blondel is making a statement fairly common throughout the history of philosophy, that is, that argument is secondary to understanding, that discourse is secondary to life. Maintaining this much is perfectly compatible with recognizing the full validity of abstract thought and argument.

The other set of problems involves the dependence of Blondel's spirituality of philosophy on his faith as a Roman Catholic and on the possibility of a culmination of action, of thought, of life in something superhuman: the grace-dependent mystical for some philosophers in this world and for all of us hereafter. What if his faith comes to seem delusional or improbable or if the mystical culmination comes to seem unlikely? Although we surely will not be Blondelians in any strong sense under these conditions, we may still share something of his spirit in the doggedness, the fairness, and the honesty with which we pursue the questions that we share with him. There will be a type of prayer in our attitude toward the world, ourselves, our projects, and possibly in our very uncertainties about all three. As Martin Heidegger once said, admittedly in an enterprise much different from Blondel's: "questioning is the piety of thought."[48]

48. Martin Heidegger, "The Question Concering Technology," in *Basic Writings*, ed. David Farrell Krell (San Francisco: HarperSanFrancisco, 1993), 341.

5 The Modernist and the Mystic

Albert Houtin's *Une grande mystique*

C. J. T. Talar

> Each of the protagonists develops a vision of this history consistent with the interests linked to the position he occupies within the history; the different historical accounts are oriented according to the position of their producer and cannot claim the status of indisputable truth.[1]

For those whose musical horizons encompass the recent revival of interest in Gregorian chant, Solesmes perhaps will not be entirely unfamiliar. The identification of this French Benedictine abbey with plainchant dates back well into the nineteenth century and its debates over how to interpret authentically the musical manuscripts of earlier eras.[2] In the course of that century, Solesmes became synonymous with the liturgical revival more broadly, its prominence dependent in no small measure on the efforts of its founder, Dom Prosper Guéranger (1805–1875).[3]

1. Pierre Bourdieu, *Science of Science and Reflexivity* (Chicago: University of Chicago Press, 2004), 9. Bourdieu continues, "One sees, in passing, one of the effects of reflexivity: what I have just said puts my listeners on their guard against what I am going to say, and puts me on my guard too, against the danger of privileging one orientation or against even the temptation to see myself as objective on the grounds for example that I am equally critical of all positions."

2. See Pierre Combe, *Histoire de la restauration du chant grégorien d'après des documents inédits* (Sablé sur Sarthe: Abbaye de Solesmes, 1969). *Restoration of Gregorian Chant: Solesmes and the Vatican Edition,* trans. Theodore N. Marier and William Skinner (Washington, D.C.: The Catholic University of America Press, 2003).

3. See Dom Olivier Rousseau, *The Progress of the Liturgy* (Westminster, Md.: The New-

Properly speaking, Guéranger restored Benedictine life at Solesmes. A priory had been established on the site in the early eleventh century and, despite natural and human disasters, monastic life continued until its suppression in 1791 under the directives of the French Revolution. As a diocesan priest, Guéranger and several companions commenced living a common life there in 1833, according to a modified Benedictine Rule, and they assumed the Benedictine habit three years later. In 1837 the constitutions received papal approval and Solesmes was raised to the status of an abbey and head of the new Benedictine congregation of France. Guéranger made his monastic profession and was appointed abbot, without having made a novitiate or been a simple monk. Thus, when Benedictine life was resumed at Solesmes, those who undertook it did not have direct experience of monastic formation. The title of founder applied to Guéranger thus is not inappropriate.[4]

Already during his seminary years Guéranger had come under the influence of the Mennasian movement and its ultramontanism. While he would distance himself from La Mennais as the latter's positions grew more extreme, the ultramontaine influence would endure. At Solesmes it found expression in the use of the Roman Missal, the Roman Breviary, support for Roman doctrines, and especially in its campaign for liturgical reform and liturgical restoration. Guéranger and Solesmes loomed large in the fight against the Gallican party in France and the adoption of the Roman rite in dioceses that followed other traditions. Guéranger saw in this effort a means both to unify the church and to counter views of religion as individualistic, moralistic, rationalistic, or nationalistic.[5]

---

man Press, 1951), ch. 1–3 and 8. Dom Delatte, third abbot of Solesmes, wrote a biography of his predecessor, *Dom Guéranger. Abbé de Solesmes*, 2 vols. (Paris: Plon-Nourrit, 1909–1910). Resolutely chronological, it makes large demands on its reader to detach and reconnect themes that developed over time. Dom Guy-Marie Oury, *Dom Guéranger. Moine au coeur de l'Église* (Solesmes: Éditions de Solesmes, 2000), was written to remedy that defect.

4. On the beginnings of Solesmes under Guéranger, see Dom Alphonse Guépin, *Solesmes et Dom Guéranger* (Le Mans: Edmond Monnoyer, 1876) and Dom Louis Soltner, *Solesmes and Dom Guéranger 1805–1895*, trans. Joseph O'Connor (Brewster, Mass.: Paraclete Press, 1995).

5. For the controversies over the restoration of the Roman liturgy in France, see R. W. Franklin, *Nineteenth-Century Churches: The History of a New Catholicism in Wüttemberg, England, and France* (New York: Garland Publishing, 1987), ch. VIII–XI; Cuthbert Johnson, *Prosper Guéranger (1805–1875): A Liturgical Theologian* (Rome: Pontificio Ateneo S. Anselmo, 1984).

While its liturgical life was central to Solesmes' living of the monastic vocation, and while study loomed large in Guéranger's vision of ecclesiastical restoration, there is manifestly an openness to the contemplative dimension of that vocation from the beginning. This element will assume greater prominence over the years, both with Guéranger himself and the Solesmes community. Over time, the Benedictine abbey ceases being a center of liturgical advancement and, accompanying a growing conservatism, increasingly turns inward toward mysticism and contemplation. The founding of a women's abbey at Solesmes in the 1860s constituted an institutional demonstration of the contemplative ideal and a further step away from the liturgical mission of the first abbey. Guéranger chose as superior of this community Jenny Bruyère (1845–1909), known in religion as Mère Cécile.[6] Together with the third abbot of Solesmes, Dom Paul Delatte (1848–1937), she figures prominently in the controversies that form the substance of Albert Houtin's study, *Une grande mystique, Madame Bruyère* (1925, 2nd ed. 1930).

In September 1887 when Albert Houtin (1867–1926) arrived at Solesmes to test his monastic vocation he found a community divided both geographically and ideologically. The French government had expelled the monks from the abbey in 1880, and again from 1882 to 1890. Although the nuns had been allowed to remain in their abbey, the monks were dispersed among the village, making common life difficult. This also created a situation of more frequent interaction between monks and nuns and of growth in the influence of the mother abbess over the monks. She exercised influence directly, through her contacts with monks who were encouraged to avail themselves of her spiritual wisdom, and indirectly through two monks who became virtually her disciples. One of the latter held the position of novice master and in that capacity served as a conduit of the teaching of one whom he regarded as a saint.[7] This occurred with the approval of the second superior of

6. See *In spiritu et veritate* (Solesmes: Sainte-Cécile de Solesmes, 1966), published on the centennial of the foundation of Sainte-Cécile.

7. Ambroise Ledru, in his *Dom Guéranger, Abbé de Solesmes et Mgr Bouvier, Évêque du Mans* (Paris: Honoré Champion, 1911), see note on 316, provides some details regarding the nature of the abbess's influence over the monks.

Solesmes, Dom Charles Couturier (1817–1890). Guéranger's successor reinforced moves away from study and scholarship, valuing such only as preparation, sustenance, and illumination of the contemplative life.[8]

In the course of his novitiate, it became apparent to Houtin that Solesmes was a community divided between the "old"—attracted by memories of the community of Saint Maur with its scholarly ideals, and the "young" with their championing of what they regarded as the true tradition of the order—the contemplative life and personal holiness. Moreover, these differences had taken on party labels, being designated the Cecilians and the anti-Cecilians, attesting to the abbess's importance. Divergence of opinion was further complicated by personal rivalry as the faction of the young was itself divided in its support of a successor to Dom Couturier between the novice master, Dom Athanase Logerot (1840–1908), and Dom Delatte, who had only recently taken vows. Moreover, these divisions were not confined to Solesmes itself, but were also present in its daughter houses at Ligugé (founded in 1853), Marseilles (1865) and Silos in Spain (1880).[9] Thus Houtin had first-hand acquaintance with the principal figures that would feature in *Une grande mystique,* as well as issues that drove their controversy.

Houtin's own sympathies were with the monastic ideals of the old. For a variety of reasons it was determined that his vocation did not lie with Solesmes and he returned to diocesan seminary, being ordained for the diocese of Angers in 1891. Although his novitiate had not been successful, over the next several years he continued to mull over the possibility of a Benedictine vocation and remained in contact with

8. A[lbert] Houtin, *Dom Couturier, Abbé de Solesmes* (Angers: Germain & G. Grassin, 1899), 211. Oury comments, "The perceptible tension at Solesmes itself and in the Congregation between pure contemplation and the intellectual apostolate at the time of Dom Delatte's abbotcy, already existed in the years following the death of Dom Guéranger." Dom Guy-Marie Oury, *Lumière et force: Mère Cécile Bruyère, première abbesse de Sainte Cécile* (Solesmes: Éditions de Solesmes, 1997), 212.

9. Albert Houtin, *Une vie de prêtre* (Paris: Rieder, 1926), ch. IV. *The Life of a Priest,* English trans. Winifred S. Whale (London: Watts & Co., 1927). Houtin identified Logerot's tenure as novice master, gained in 1879 with the support of Sainte-Cécile, as the dividing line between those formed earlier, the "old," and those he formed, the "young." Albert Houtin, "Notes sur les profès de l'abbaye de Solesmes," in *La Province du Maine* XIX (1911): 167–73, 191–98, 229–38, 271–77, 292–95, 327–33, 361–67, 385–91, at 367.

Benedictine life at Silos and at Solesmes. He was able to follow closely the events he would later bring into print.

In reality, *Une grande mystique* is made up of two texts. By far the greater part consists of a memorandum written in 1891 by a monk of Solesmes, Dom Joseph Sauton (1856–1916), setting forth for the Holy Office certain alleged abuses he experienced that compromised monastic life at the two abbeys. A major share of the responsibility for the deviations he placed on Mère Cécile Bruyère. The memorandum he communicated to the Holy Office in April of 1892 consisted of four parts: an historical section setting forth events leading up to the election of Dom Delatte as abbot in 1890, a theological evaluation of the mystical phenomena claimed by the abbess, a medico-psychological evaluation of her family background and behavior, and a final section noting the state of affairs at Solesmes in 1891. In the first edition of *Une grande mystique* Houtin exercised discretion and did not publish the third portion of Sauton's text. After Houtin's death, his literary executor, Félix Sartiaux, decided to include it in a second edition.[10] In both editions the memorandum is prefaced by a biography of Bruyère which takes the narrative beyond the point reached by Sauton's memorandum.

Sauton's Solesmes

> As [Erving] Goffman argues, narrators assume a wide range of roles in narratives. . . . The narrator can move between such guises as a participant in the narrated events, an eyewitness to their unfolding, a commentator on their social and historical location, an observer who can trace what happened later, an interpreter who can tell why events took a particular course, and a participant in the ongoing, narrative event who can thus point to the significance of these events for the narrating event.[11]

10. Albert Houtin, *Une grande mystique. Madame Bruyère* (Paris: Félix Alcan, 1925, 2nd ed., 1930). Sauton eventually left monastic life, taking up the practice of medicine in which he had been trained. It was his desire that his memorandum be published after his death. He confided it to Mgr Mignot, archbishop of Albi, for that purpose. After Sauton's death in 1916, Mignot decided that his position as archbishop prevented publication under his auspices, and he passed it on to Houtin. While well aware that some of the protagonists were yet living, he judged it possible to publish the text Sauton had conserved, inviting those with first-hand knowledge of the circumstances to "furnish their recollections and their documents" (vi).

11. Charles L. Briggs, introduction to *Disorderly Discourse: Narrative, Conflict, and Inequality*, ed. Charles L. Briggs (Oxford: Oxford University Press, 1996), 26–27.

After completion of medical studies and a period of several years spent working with nervous and mental illnesses in Paris, Joseph Sauton became a postulant at Solesmes in 1884. He was then twenty-seven-years old. Dom Couturier presided over a monastic community living under anomalous conditions, dispersed outside the abbey. Dom Logerot presided over the novices, and it soon became apparent to Sauton that he saw Mère Cécile as the exemplar of the monastic life and the continuator of Dom Guéranger's spirit, more than the abbot. For Logerot, the abbess "is the personification of the Church, whose fate has been placed in her hands." The theory of vicarious suffering, prominent in French spirituality at the time, is manifest in his conviction that the voluntary acceptance of her "physical and moral sufferings" plays no small role in resisting the trials and tribulations visited upon the Church. She is credited with the gift of bilocation, which enables her to assist those at Rome with decisions affecting the Church's well being; she possesses the gift of clairvoyance; she can perform miracles; "in a word, this is the greatest saint of modern times."[12]

Despite these encomiums of the abbess as "an extraordinary mystic, an eminent saint," Sauton was not initially converted to Logerot's views.[13] Nor did he think the frequenting of Saint-Cécile by his fellow novices was prudent practice. At several points in his narrative it is apparent that there also are underlying gender issues.[14] Sauton rejected Bruyère's claims to have received from Guéranger on his deathbed the care of his monastic sons and daughters as a solemn mandate. The abbot could not have meant this, he insisted, for "he, more than any other, respected the plan of God, who places power in the hands of men: the mission of women is carried out in other areas."[15] All the more so when it is a matter of male hierarchy: priesthood, abbecy, direction of the congregation.[16] Despite Logerot's open veneration of the abbess and

12. Houtin, *Une grande mystique,* 94–95. Note: the pagination of the 1925 and 1930 editions are identical where Houtin's introduction, and parts 1, 2, and 4 of Sauton's memorandum are concerned. Sartiaux added part 3 as an appendix, covering pages 311–44. Hereafter, page references will refer to the more complete 1930 edition.

13. Ibid., 86.

14. It is also apparent from Houtin's comments in his introductory pages that he is of one mind with Sauton on these matters.

15. Houtin, *Une grande mystique,* 88.

16. Ibid., 88; cf. 99–100.

Couturier's esteem for her spiritual attainments, Sauton kept his distance, which was reciprocated by a coldness on Bruyère's side.

After Sauton's monastic profession in 1885, this state of affairs underwent a transformation. His service as a doctor brought him into closer relations with Sainte-Cécile and its superior, softening his impressions of Mère Cécile. Further, the abbot's urgings that the abbess could be of substantial assistance to Sauton's spiritual progress began to have their effect. In effect, Bruyère's sanctity altered his perception of her femininity: "it was not a woman but a saint with whom I was going to speak, a saint divested of the weaknesses of her sex, a saint clothed with the title and the rarest privileges that the Son of God deigned to accord those whom he named as his spouses, etc."[17] In May of 1886, with requisite docility, he placed himself under the abbesses's direction.

If according the mother abbess an aura of sanctity did much to alter his perception of her feminine status, it did not as readily transform his monastic ideals. Her language of spiritual maternity, designating Sauton her "beloved little child," brought through a "mystical death" to a "new birth" and receiving in consequence a new name, her "dear little Tibertius"[18] nursed "at her breast" and nourished with "a virginal milk,"[19] stood at odds with his militant image of the monk as a disciplined, virile knight of the holy church.[20] Through acts of will he suppressed such thoughts, but could not banish them entirely. Nor could the doctor trained in psychopathology be set entirely at rest.

In yet other ways Sauton experienced cognitive dissonance, based on Bruyère's claims to spiritual favors, and the patterns of her behavior that he witnessed over time. He reproduces textually two accounts of Bruyère's spiritual favors, dating from the 1870s, which described her visions of Christ and his Blessed Mother, going into fine detail over their

17. Ibid., 100.

18. In the hagiographical legends surrounding Saint Cecilia, Tibertius was the brother of her husband, Valerian. The two brothers were converted through her intercession and both were martyred during Roman persecution. See Dom Prosper Guéranger, *Histoire de sainte Cécile* (Tournai: J. Casterman, 1851), ch. VI-X. English trans. *Life of Saint Cecilia* (Philadelphia: Peter F. Cunningham, 1866).

19. Houtin, *Une grande mystique*, 120–22.

20. Ibid., 105.

respective appearances.[21] In the latter case, through a communication beyond words, "by a kind of mutual compenetration" Mary shared the joys of her own virginal motherhood.[22] To Sauton directly the abbess declared that she received an apparition of Christ who informed her, despite her conviction that it was in the eternal plan of God that she would soon join her Lord and Spouse in his heavenly kingdom, that her presence on earth was still required. Later in his narrative Sauton reveals the importance she attributed to that continuing earthly exile. At the death of Cardinal Pie in 1880 she pronounced, "Three of the four columns of the Church are no longer: Dom Guéranger, Cardinal Pie and Pius IX. And yet God cannot let it be borne only by me." To which he comments, "The sole column which remained standing was not Leo XIII, but rather the Madam Abbess of Sainte-Cécile, both Cecilian monks and nuns repeating with no less emotion than conviction: 'Madam Abbess carries and supports the entire edifice of the Church.'"[23] Her "sublime mission," subject to the fierce assaults of the Devil, who "saw in her the most redoubtable enemy," required more than the ordinary run of guardian angel. Sauton reports, "The Lord had to this effect delegated Saint Michael to her, with whom she lived in a constant familiarity, and all the other angels that comprised his cortège." To him she avowed, "How lovely are all these angels, my little Tibertius. They flutter about me unceasingly, causing me to hear celestial concerts; sometimes they even deafen me to the point that I am obliged to impose silence upon them." Apparently Dom Logerot's credulity went so far as to impute Bruyère's treatise on prayer to angelic dictation, at such rate that she could scarcely keep up with it![24]

Such are a sampling of the claims to extraordinary sanctity. On several occasions, however, the abbess's character struck a discordant note with Sauton. He cites several incidents of her breaking confidentiality, both his and others. The abbots of the daughter houses and Dom Couturier himself were not immune to negative characterizations by her.[25] In short, she undermined others in order to exalt herself.

21. Ibid., 131–33, 134–35.

22. Ibid., 134.

23. Ibid., 237.

24. Ibid., 130–31.

25. Ibid., 118–20.

In light of these behaviors the doctor reemerged to question the monk. But the doctor could also find mitigating circumstances: her aberrations were the effects of an unhealthy heredity. However, the doctor could not simply confine himself to exculpatory diagnosis. The "beloved child" became the "devoted son" as he sought to express his concerns to his spiritual mother.[26]

Bruyère's reaction to Sauton's concerns induced a crisis into their relationship:

> Until then I never thought that she had anything more than a defective organic constitution leading to the strange need to lie and to toss out spiteful insinuations about others. Such disorders were serious, but still could be reconciled, if need be, with a degree of sanctification above the ordinary.[27]

The ferocity of her response and the pride it manifested, however, were the very negation of sanctity. All this took place close to Sauton's ordination to priesthood, which occurred in March of 1888. Around that time he became aware of a campaign conducted by the abbess with the intent of undermining him in the eyes of the monks, the nuns, and even those outside the monastery.[28] A rift had been created and it would not be bridged.

Thus Sauton joined the ranks of the anti-Cecelians. The abbess had earlier wielded her influence to secure the appointment of Dom Logerot as novice master. In the interval Henri Delatte (in religion Paul) had entered Solesmes and in him she discerned Guéranger's true successor.[29] At Dom Couturier's death in 1890 she worked to secure Delatte's elec-

26. Ibid., 152.

27. Ibid., 153.

28. Sauton's marginalization in the Solesmes' community was observed by Houtin during the year of his novitiate. *Une grande mystique*, n. 43.

29. Olis Henri Delatte entered Solesmes in 1883 and made his monastic profession in 1885. His rise within the community was rapid; by 1888 he had become prior and, during Dom Couturier's last illnesses, virtual abbot. In his autobiography Houtin describes the circumstances of Delatte's election. "I heard that the election had not taken place without considerable difficulty and many regrettable incidents. The rivalry between 'the young' and 'the old,' far from diminishing, had become complicated by all sorts of questions. One of the new Abbot's first acts was to relegate the other candidate of 'the young,' who was his rival but also his former master, Dom Logerot, to a monastery which was considered the depository of Solesmes." Houtin, *Vie*, 120; *Life*, 69.

tion as abbot. His success in attaining that position further alienated Sauton.

Having set forth his relations with Mère Cécile, Sauton, in the second part of his memorandum interprets her claims to sanctity and mystical experience from a theological perspective. Reference has already been made in passing to a treatise on prayer written by the abbess. In 1885 she began writing *De l'Oraison,* destined originally for the nuns of Sainte-Cécile. Later enlarged, it was published and circulated under the title, *La vie spirituelle et l'oraison.*[30] It was not employed by Sauton as an object of direct theological analysis, however, as in general he found it to be in harmony with the Church's doctrine.[31] Instead, he based his theological critique on her private revelations of her mystical experiences—and found in them an entirely different person than the one manifested in the published work.

He begins this section with a retrieval of the classic teaching on the possible sources of mystical phenomena: they may be divine, diabolical or naturalistic in origin. He then proceeds to test her visions and revelations against these possibilities. Given the historical importance of visions as warrants for the authority of women mystics, and their salience for Bruyère herself, attention will be confined to his evaluation of them.[32] The two visions reported textually in the first, historical part—those of Christ and his Mother—are retrieved here for theological examination.

As an initial step, Sauton categorizes them theologically as "imaginary visions,"[33] that is, "a sensible representation, circumscribed within the limits of the imagination, and which presents itself naturally to the mind with as much vivacity and clarity as physical realities themselves."[34] Given the non-corporeal status of the objects of this type of vision, these experiences are very subject to illusion. If the visions are

30. English trans. *The Spiritual Life and Prayer* [1900] (Eugene, Or.: Wipf and Stock, 2002).

31. Houtin, *Une grande mystique,* 236.

32. See Grace M. Jantzen, *Power, Gender and Christian Mysticism* (Cambridge: Cambridge University Press, 1995), ch. 5 especially.

33. Visions may also be corporeal or intellectual (cf. 200–202). Sauton gives the text of one of Bruyère's intellectual visions on page 136 and later subjects it to analysis (214–15).

34. Houtin, *Une grande mystique,* 201.

naturalistic in origin, visionaries could deceive themselves. If the origin is supernatural, they may have been deceived by a demon. It is therefore necessary to have recourse to the mystical theological tradition to judge whether such visions may be divine.

The visionary experiences of Christ as reported by Saint Teresa serve as a touchstone of comparison with Bruyère's. For the Carmelite, such interior visions stimulate in the soul an attraction above itself, imprint an image which leaves a deep and lasting impression on the mind, and produce fruits of grace in the soul. For the spiritual masters, there is agreement that such recipients, were they to draw attention to themselves by repeatedly proclaiming the graces with which they have been favored, show by such practices either the natural origin or the diabolical inspiration of their experiences.[35]

On all of these counts the Benedictine abbess's vision fails to measure up. Hers confines itself to a description of Christ's appearance, the work of a literary artist adept at surface impressions that fail to convey the intellectual and moral beauty of the God-man. While finely wrought in its detail, the overall effect is literary: an exercise in style, leaving an impression less striking than would viewing some devotional image. Moreover, far from keeping an edifying reticence, she made copies of her vision available to the monks and nuns.

Bruyère's second vision of Our Lady manifests the same defects. In addition, Sauton notes that the communication revolves around the themes of spiritual maternity that so preoccupied the abbess. In the guise of being about the Mother of Christ, it is in reality about the mother abbess. Visions rather are to lead to the grandeur, the holiness of God. "Mystical theologians are also in agreement in not admitting, as divine supernatural, wonders whose object would be sterile, childish or grotesque."[36]

After proceeding to evaluate an intellectual vision she reported, accounts of revelations she received, her powers of discernment regarding aptitude for a monastic vocation and for progress in the mystical life, and noting once again her lack of the virtues that constitute

35. Ibid., 202–5.
36. Ibid., 211.

both foundation and the fruit of a true mysticism, he concludes that her experiences were natural in origin rather than supernatural.[37] The combination of the facts he reviewed and the theological authorities he cited render impossible a divine character to the various prodigies examined.[38]

In the third part of the memorandum, the doctor, never very distant, moves to the forefront and renders his diagnosis, laying bare the basis upon which Bruyère's mysticism truly rests. Although part of his clinical experience was gained at the Salpêtrière under Jean-Martin Charcot, Sauton is no reductionist. In his view medical science needs to maintain a certain humility in face of the supernatural, while retaining a utility in detecting illusion or stimulation that proceeds from unhealthy psychic conditions.[39] The line between the natural and supernatural is, in the very nature of things, difficult to trace. But the supernatural, divine or diabolical, cannot simply be ruled out. He does note that in his own clinical experience he never encountered "any sign that disclosed a diabolical intervention."[40]

The fascination with the influence of heredity evident in latter nineteenth-century literature, such as Émile Zola's Rougon-Macquart cycle of novels, surfaces here. An examination of Mère Cécile's family of origin reveals a legacy of nervous disequilibrium and hysteria, which leave their mark on Jenny Bruyère's own childhood and adolescence.

Hysterics can be divided into three classes: those whose symptoms are purely somatic, those whose symptoms are exclusively psychic, and those who exhibit a combination of the two. In Bruyère he finds an example of the second type, or "moral form" of hysteria.[41] A psychological study of the abbess yields evidence of the salient traits of this type. The first trait of such hysterics is mobility, in the sense of rapid transitions from joy to sadness, from laughter to tears. Their inconstancy is a constant. In the preceding sections of his narrative Sauton had several times described for his readers such abrupt changes observed in the course of his encounters with her. Second, hysterics possess a spirit

37. Ibid., 215.
38. Ibid., 213.
39. Ibid., 315.
40. Ibid., 314.
41. Ibid., 319.

of opposition and contradiction, which surfaces in Bruyère's taking positions to the extreme, either affirming or denying them according to momentary whim or fantasy. Third, such hysterics exhibit a spirit of duplicity. In Bruyère's case, Sauton notes the contrast between the words of tenderness to her "well beloved sons" spoken to their face, in contrast to marking their tiniest faults and shortcomings behind their backs. She lies, as seen in her broken promises of confidentiality surrounding their written and spoken interchanges. And she simulates—emerging in her claims to "bilocation, mystical illness, commerce with the Angels and Saints, virginal maternity," and also in her claims to complete abstention from any involvement in the election of Dom Delatte as abbot, all evidence to the contrary notwithstanding. Fourth, hysterics display pride and egoism. Bruyère, he notes, had a need to communicate her spiritual favors, and her self-exaltation as the self-designated guardian of Guéranger's legacy at Solesmes and indeed as surviving supporting column of the entire church. Fifth, hysterics displayed an excitability that could assume the form of an "erotic mania." Bruyère manifested this characteristic in her spiritual maternity that infantized adults by claiming to nurse them spiritually at their mother's breast, and expressed in a language of voluptuous imagery that concealed passions under a "virginal veil." Finally, hysterics often have a hyperactive intellect, compensating for an attenuated affectivity in a fertile imagination, a facile pen, in animated conversation.[42]

The comparison of these hysterical traits with the unpublished writings and observed behaviors of Mère Cécile "imposes on the doctor the diagnosis of moral hysteria with complications of a veritable mystic and erotic mania [*délire*]." He notes that mystical delusion is nearly always accompanied by erotic delusion—"a recognized fact in mental pathology."[43] The theological analysis of Mère Cécile's mystical claims could not sustain a divine origin for those. The medical analysis established to Sauton's satisfaction their true source: a sick organism whose overfertile imagination gave birth to multiple illusions.

The fourth and final part of Sauton's narrative may be dealt with

42. Ibid., 324–42.
43. Ibid., 342.

summarily. In it he seeks to draw out the dangerous consequences of a spirituality founded on illusion for monastic life and tradition. Not long after his election Dom Delatte opens negotiations with government officials for the reoccupation of the abbey by the monks, and succeeds in these designs. But the price is high. He is perceived to have capitulated to the demands of the anti-clerical government, thereby compromising Solesmes's reputation of principled resistance, to have broken with the tradition of his predecessor and to have betrayed the legacy of the abbey's founder. This introduces elements of strain between the new superior and other abbots of the congregation in the daughter houses. Also contributing in no small measure to these tensive relations is the prominent role the abbess was seen to play in the abbey's affairs. This perception further undermines support that Solesmes had enjoyed from benefactors.

Moreover, Delatte's regime exacerbates internal tensions within the community. It was a matter, for Sauton, of the monastery reaping what the abbess had sown: "cliques, numerous parties which fed malicious gossip, calumnies, competitions, jealousies."[44] Examples were supplied. Moreover, he portrayed the abbot as capricious and contradictory in his directives, autocrat rather than paterfamialias. Nor, when compared with the elements identified by Guéranger as constituting the essence of the monastic life, did Delatte's teaching conform. On the contrary, he had positively transformed some of these elements, to the detriment of the quality of life experienced by the community and compromising the monastic tradition. Paramount among these tenets was the exalted role accorded to contemplation, reflecting yet again the hand of Mère Cécile.[45] Problems being experienced by the abbey were traced to their source, the "false spirituality that comes to us from Sainte-Cécile."[46] Sauton brings his narrative to a close by considering the likelihood that

44. Ibid., 253.

45. There is also the matter of the exalted role accorded the mother abbess. He warns: "It is not without impunity that one ignores the plan of God in the hierarchy that he has established and, when monks clothed with the priestly character place themselves under the spiritual direction of a woman, they launch themselves onto a path full of dangers, while removing themselves from the laws of the Church, and will only end up powerless." All the more so when the woman in question manifests mental illness. *Une grande mystique,* 268.

46. Ibid.

Delatte would recognize the danger posed to Solesmes and its source, and he gives several reasons to conclude in the negative.

Sauton terminated his memorandum in December of 1891. In Houtin's introduction the thread of the narrative is picked up and carried forward to Bruyère's death in 1909. If Sauton's memorandum created something of an interpretive problem for later readers trying to gain an accurate assessment of Bruyère and her mystical claims, it had more immediate repercussions for Solesmes, Dom Delatte, and Mère Cécile herself. Sauton drafted his memorandum after being sent by Delatte to Ligugé in 1891, part of an attempt on the abbot's part to lessen tensions in the community. The memorandum, accompanied by supporting documentation, was actually conveyed to Rome in April of 1892.[47] It was not until the following year that the Holy Office took decisive action. Delatte was suspended from his functions as abbot and ordered to reside at Subiaco, while an interim replacement governed in his stead. All relations between the two abbeys were interdicted, with the nuns at Sainte-Cécile being placed under the jurisdiction of the local bishop and diocesan priests replacing the monks as their confessors. Although these measures were not publicized, word leaked out and grew into rumors of improper conduct between the abbess and the abbot. Others, more moderate, believed the affair to be confined to matters involving mysticism, interpreting it as a resurgence of quietism with the abbess as a new Madame Guyon.

In his narrative of these events, Houtin laconically observes, "The Benedictines, seeing their superior menaced, did not confine themselves to prayer and other mystical means to save her."[48] Among the community of nuns at Sainte-Cécile were members of royalty who used their family connections to solicit Emperor Franz Joseph and Queen Christina of Spain to intervene on Solesmes's behalf directly with Leo XIII. The outcome was a transformation of a juridical and doctrinal process before the Holy Office into a papally sanctioned diplomatic solution. The apostolic visitor sent to Solesmes conducted his inquiry so as to yield

47. The circumstances surrounding the generation of Sauton's memorandum, as well as a second authored by Dom Martin de La Tremblaye (1856–1909), are recorded by Houtin, *Une grande mystique*, 54–56.

48. Ibid., 61.

conclusions favorable to the pope's desires, leading to Delatte's reinstatement late in 1893.[49]

Other Solesmes

> When a narrative is embedded in an ongoing conflict, analysts are unlikely to assume a one-to-one relationship between accounts and the events they are taken to portray. Nowhere is it more likely that there will be at least two sides to every story, neither of which can be taken as objective. The indeterminacy inherent in narrative representation may not be immediately evident in many contexts, but it cannot be avoided in cases of conflict.[50]

Houtin prided himself on his objectivity as an historian, many times reiterated in his historical and biographical writings, and repeatedly reaffirmed in his autobiography. But he was personally involved in the story he tells. His autobiography, *Une vie de prêtre,* traces the impact on him of the intellectual renaissance Catholicism was experiencing toward the close of the century. Houtin became an active participant in the movement for the renewal eventually condemned in 1907 as Modernism, an involvement which ultimately led to the loss of his faith and his openly leaving the Church in 1912. Among the documents published by Sartiaux as part of the second volume of Houtin's autobiography, *Ma vie laïque,* were some pages on his experiences with the Benedictines. He admits that it was only over the course of a number of years that he came to know "the details of the abbess's aberrations," that he came to appreciate "the force, the subtlety, the captivating charm, the insincerity, the morbidity of mystics, their power of auto-suggestion and the strength of their illuminism, their pious barefaced lies, their churchy cabals, all protected and concealed by ecclesiastical authority."[51] Houtin had come a long way from the young, idealistic novice that had arrived at Solesmes in 1887 to embrace the monastic life. For the freethinker that he had become, "Solesmes was a very significant experience of my life, a lived and living proof of the Christian illusion."[52]

49. This brief recapitulation glosses over the complexities surrounding these measures. Houtin goes into greater detail regarding them.

50. Donald Brenneis, "Telling Troubles: Narrative, Conflict, and Experience," in *Disorderly Discourse,* ed. Briggs, 42.

51. Albert Houtin, *Ma vie laïque* (Paris: Rieder, 1928), 118.

52. Ibid., 118–19.

Thus when he published *Une grande mystique* in 1925, Houtin would have allowed only one possible source of mystical experience: naturalistic illusion. He acknowledged that mystics presented a special sort of challenge: if knowledge of any soul is difficult, that of a mystic is especially so. In the case of the "great enigmas" that are the mystics, it is not possible to claim "definitive explanation" of their psychology. Nonetheless, it is equally clear that Houtin published Sauton's memorandum as documentation in anticipation of his history of the Benedictine Congregation of Solesmes. Though that history would treat Madame Bruyère only briefly, he expected his treatment would cause sufficient surprise to benefit from the support of Sauton's testimony.[53] He hoped, that is, that with Sauton's support he could offer a reasonably definitive explanation of Bruyère's mysticism. Moreover, he, unlike Sauton, viewed Bruyère as representative of the defects of Christian mysticism more generally.

Some found Houtin's publication of Sauton's memorandum helpful. In his review of *Une grande mystique* Alfred Loisy judged the memorandum to be "written with extreme candor and great care for exactness, a great deal of moderation in its judgments," constituting a record of the day by day, intimate life of two monasteries.[54] Though not altogether hostile to mysticism as a phenomenon of human life, Loisy's positive judgment on an exposé of Catholic life at the end of the nineteenth century is perhaps not surprising in light of his 1908 excommunication. The relationship between Loisy and Houtin was complex, but they agreed at least in their suspicion of the Catholic hierarchy.

Predictably, others were more critical. Jean Baruzi, whose *Jean de la Croix et le problème de l'expérience mystique* appeared one year earlier than Houtin's book on Bruyère, did not question Sauton's sincerity in his review. But, he insisted, it could not deliver a proven judgment, given the very character of the document as a denunciation addressed to the Holy Office. Rather it opened up a problem requiring further investigation, an inquiry that would require examination of the autobiog-

53. Ibid., v–vii.

54. Alfred Loisy, review of *Une grande mystique* in *Revue critique d'histoire et de littérature* (1 July 1925): 243–45, at 244.

raphy, the journal of Bruyère's mystical life, and letters that remained inaccessible to the historian. Despite its author's desires, Baruzi concluded, *Une grande mystique* does not supply the data that would be necessary to render an exact image of its subject. "When all is said and done, we are insufficiently informed to study as psychologists, and even as historians, Mme Bruyère's case."[55]

Henri Delacroix shared judgments reached by Baruzi, but was able to develop them at greater length in the course of a long review article in the *Journal de psychologie normale et pathologique.* Delacroix notes that Houtin had granted him access to the pages of the third, medico-psychological part of the memorandum, which he decided to suppress due to the delicate nature of its contents. But Sauton's medico-psychological diagnosis was all the more reason to regret not being able to consult Bruyère's unpublished writings, especially her "Comptes rendus de conscience," since Sauton had based his medical diagnoses in significant measure upon them. Delacroix queries, "In all sincerity, would we be able to establish an intimate history of Mme. Guyon by relying solely on Bossuet?"

Beyond the very character of the document itself, there are Sauton's own evident limitations. "Blinded by his feelings of rancor, by his instinctive and acquired distrust, and by the medical biases that he had acquired in the climate created by Charcot's work," his testimony must be taken as precisely that—testimony, and not veridical history.[56] In short, the diagnosis is not only about the clinical subject but can also reveal much about the diagnostician. For example, in Delacroix's estimation Sauton's reading of Jenny Bruyère's behavior during her adolescent years as confirming the presence of hysteria betrays a lack of fa-

55. Jean Baruzi, review of *Une grande mystique in Revue philosophique* (March–April 1926): 310–12, at 312. Baruzi's *Saint Jean de la Croix et le problème de l'expérience mystique* has recently been republished (Paris: Éditions Salvator, 1999) with an introduction by Émile Poulat. See also Poulat's *L'Université devant la mystique* (Paris: Éditions Salvator, 1999). Baruzi succeeded Loisy at the Collège de France in 1931.

56. H. Delacroix, "Remarques sur 'Une grande mystique,'" *Journal de psychologie normale et pathologique* (July 15, 1925): 545–84, at 555–56. Delacroix's *Études d'histoire et de psychologie du mysticisme. Les grandes mystiques chrétiens* (Paris: Félix Alcan, 1908) shows him as sympathetic interpreter of mysticism. Although attributing a naturalistic origin to mystical experience, the achievements of its great representatives argued against a reduction to psychopathology.

miliarity with what is normally to be expected in the development of young women. On the other hand, his close familiarity with Charcot's work narrows his clinical approach. Hysteria possessed in 1884 a clarity of diagnosis based on a firm set of traits that later clinical practice would call into question, as it would the close linkage between mystical phenomena and psychopathology.

Delacroix concedes that, if there are hysterics, there can be religious hysterics. But he also argues that mystical phenomena can proceed from valid, if intense, religious experience, experience of an intensity that may well find expression in the kinds of excesses, the "mystical extravagances" that Sauton describes. But for all that a valid intensity, accompanied by deeply held beliefs, a lively imagination and an emotivity that are consonant with a legitimate type of religiosity rather than mental disorder. "Sauton was astonished that a spiritual doctrine as sober as the abbess's could coexist with such an efflorescence of external demonstrations. On the contrary, we have attempted to show that this combination is frequent among the mystics and that the very nature of their spiritual enterprise requires it so."[57]

Conclusion

As noted earlier, narratives can exhibit a certain ambiguity, particularly in the case of conflict narratives. Conceptually, theorists distinguish between "narrative events"—the discursive portrayal—and "narrated events"—the words and actions that are related. Thus, "narratives do not simply describe ready-made events, they provide central means by which we *create* notions as to what took place, how the action unfolded, what prompted it, and the social effects of the events."[58] Both Baruzi and Delacroix show greater awareness of these issues in their respective reviews of the Houtin and Sauton renditions than do Houtin and Sauton themselves. As does the biography of Mère Cécile authored by Dom Guy-Marie Oury of Solesmes, which tells a different story.

Oury acknowledges that Houtin's book has been influential in shap-

57. Delacroix, "Remarques sur 'Une grande mystique,'" 582.

58. Briggs, introduction in *Disorderly Discourse,* ed. Briggs, 22–23.

ing perceptions of Solesmes over the period it describes,[59] but challenges it as "a version systematically unfavorable to Solesmes, to Dom Delatte and to Mère Cécile." Its author's motives are questioned, since "he had a score to settle with the hierarchical Church, with the condemnations that had struck the group of Modernists to which he had belonged, and with all of the Christian company that he had known in the period of his clerical youth."[60] Beyond such direct challenges to the adequacy of *Une grande mystique,* attentive reading of Oury's biography suggests that Houtin's narrative is never very far from the Benedictine's mind. While he could not claim the participant role shared by Houtin and Sauton, Oury could function as commentator and interpreter, thereby shaping the significance of narrated events.

He adopts several strategies to make his case. Already at a young age Jenny Bruyère came under Dom Guéranger's direction. At his insistence she then, and for long after her religious profession, recorded her spiritual experiences. Oury retrieves a description of her prayer life dating from 1862, when she was not yet seventeen, that shows her already well advanced along the way of prayer, the recipient of "graces of mystical character."[61] Supporting the textual evidence provided by Bruyère's own writings, there are the judgments made by Guéranger himself, who had intimate knowledge of her interior life over a considerable period. Attentive not only to her words, but also to "the fruits that these graces produced in her life," he saw in her the makings of a saint.[62]

59. As a notable example, in his biography of the novelist Joris-Karl Huysmans, James Laver accepts Houtin's version of events in providing context for Huysmans's relations with Delatte and Bruyère while in the process of discerning a possible Benedictine vocation. See James Laver, *The First Decadent* (New York: Citadel Press, 1955), ch. 11.

60. Guy-Marie Oury, *Lumière et force: Mère Cécile* (Solesmes: Éditions de Solesmes, 2005), 286. Oury acknowledged that Houtin's 1899 biography of Dom Couturier remains a good reference work. But his later biographical notes on the professed at Solesmes are representative of his style. "They are nearly uniformly negative and partial," more caricature than characterization (286, 288). Houtin could be severe on those whose positions diverged from his own, as is evident from his judgments on some of his former fellow Modernists in *Ma vie laïque,* part II.

61. "I cannot apply my mind to any subject during prayer, at present, she wrote on August 17, 1862, because immediately when I pray, my heart is turned toward Our Savior with so ardent a love that all other thought is impossible for me, at least insofar as it is not directly related, such as zeal for the salvation of souls for example." Oury, *Lumière et force,* 72. Cf. 83.

62. Ibid., 83.

Thus part of Oury's task, beyond that of establishing the validity of Bruyère's mystical experiences on the basis of her own writings, is to affirm the credibility of assessments by Guéranger and others. The abbot was no stranger to the illusions that could arise in the spiritual life, nor were his successors, Couturier and Delatte, oblivious to the dangers of a false mysticism. Oury emphasizes that "all three recognized in Mère Cécile the authentic mark of God's action. They will not be the only ones; other great spirituals have come into contact with her and have reached the same conclusion."[63] Throughout the course of the biography, then, Oury is solicitous to show his subject as exemplar of an authentic, well-grounded spirituality that served as a secure foundation for the divine favors she received.

Central to all of these accounts with their varied perspectives is the understanding of mysticism that informs each of them. Sauton represents a view common among Catholics at the end of the nineteenth century that mysticism was an authentic part of the Christian tradition, but it remained the privilege of an elite few who had dramatic encounters with God. Particular claims to mystical experiences were to be greeted with caution, as they could in reality be manifestations of some underlying psychological pathology. The latter perspective informs the "narrated events" that form the substance of Sauton's memorandum. Houtin appreciated the suspicion of Catholic authors toward mystical claims, but generalized that suspicion to encompass the entire mystical tradition itself. Sauton's false mysticism becomes identified with all mysticism. By the time Houtin published his book, however, many intellectuals, Catholic and not, had moved away from this understanding of the mystical state, as exemplified in the sympathetic responses to mystical experience by Delacroix and Baruzi. Lastly, from a different view of the contemplative life, there emerges in the pages of Oury's biography a portrait of Cécile Bruyère very different from the one that dominates *Une grande mystique.*

Given this study's focus on Albert Houtin's *Une grande mystique,* equal attention has not been paid to Oury's narrative of Mère Cécile's

63. Ibid., 123.

life experiences. Enough, hopefully, to validate the choice of Pierre Bourdieu's observations that serve as this paper's epigraph. These pages are not, however, simply intended as another exercise in postmodernist ambiguity. As both Baruzi and Delacroix recognized in the course of their reviews, and Oury in his biography of Mère Cécile, Sauton's memorandum and Houtin's framing of it serve indexical functions, granting access to an historically situated clinical perspective on the one hand, and a radically positivist epistemology of religious experience on the other.

6 Henri Bergson and Alfred Loisy

On Mysticism and the Religious Life

Harvey Hill

Many Catholics around the turn of the twentieth century viewed appeals to religious experience as suspect. After all, Protestants often emphasized religious experience over against the objective truths enunciated by the Catholic Church through the centuries. And looming behind the Protestant emphasis on experience was the even more fearsome specter of Kantian subjectivism, the idea that all truth was relative to the knower. In response, many Catholic intellectuals turned to neo-Thomistic philosophy and theology, which were believed to provide a solid foundation for a properly orthodox Christian faith in properly deferential lay Christians.

But not all Catholics shared this distrust of religious experience. Those who would later be identified and condemned as Modernists by Pope Pius X, as well as a number of their fellow travelers, argued that appeals to religious experience were consistent with fidelity to the Catholic tradition. Their heroes were the mystics and the spiritual writers, not the theologians, and many insisted that neo-Thomism without reference to religious experience was an empty abstraction, divorced from the reality of Christian life. The task, they believed, was to use modern religious experience to enliven traditional Catholic teaching so that the Church could remain a vital religious force in the modern world.[1]

Among those Modernists who appealed to religious experience was Alfred Loisy (1857–1940), a priest and biblical scholar who sought to combine his two vocations until he was excommunicated in 1908. After his excommunication, Loisy continued his scholarly work in the secular academy, but religious controversy continued to dog him. Attacked from both his left and his right as a closet rationalist who had remained in the Church under false pretenses, Loisy defended the integrity of his Christian faith before his excommunication and his consistency thereafter in a series of autobiographies.[2] Loisy had defenders as well, including Henri Bremond (1865–1933), a priest and noted scholar of Christian mysticism. In *Un clerc qui n'a pas trahi,* Bremond presented Loisy as a mystic of sorts.[3] Loisy, who worked with Bremond on his book, approved of this description of himself. But even while still a Catholic, Loisy was not a mystic in the commonly understood sense of that term, and he was not widely regarded as having mystical sensibilities. As Émile Poulat notes, "the Critic and the Mystic are often presented as the faces of Modernism, illustrated by the contrasting figures

1. Recent histories of Modernism include Marvin O'Connell, *Critics on Trial: An Introduction to the Catholic Modernist Crisis* (Washington, D.C.: The Catholic University of America Press, 1994), and Pierre Colin, *L'audace et le soupçon: La crise moderniste dans le catholicisme français (1893–1914)* (Paris: Desclée de Brouwer, 1997).

2. In 1980 Ronald Burke surveyed the various opinions about Loisy's sincerity and articulated what appears to be the consensus: that Loisy had at least a "Catholic kind of faith" during his Catholic years. See "Loisy's Faith: Landshift in Catholic Thought," *Journal of Religion* 60 (1980): 138–64. The most important of Loisy's autobiographies are *Choses passées* (Paris: Émile Nourry, 1913) and *Mémoires pour servir à l'histoire religieuse de notre temps,* 3 vols. (Paris: Émile Nourry, 1930–1931). On the similarities and differences in them, see Harvey Hill, "More Than a Biblical Critic: Alfred Loisy's Modernism in Light of His Autobiographies," in *Personal Faith and Institutional Commitments: Roman Catholic Modernist and Anti-Modernist Autobiography,* ed. Lawrence Barmann and Harvey Hill (Scranton, Penn.: University of Scranton Press, 2002), and in shorter form, in *Anglican Theological Review* 85 (2003): 689–707.

3. *Une Œuvre clandestine d'Henri Bremond: Sylvain LeBlanc, Un Clerc qui n'a pas trahi: Alfred Loisy d'après ses Mémoires,* ed. Émile Poulat (Roma: Edizioni di Storia e Letteratura, 1972). Bremond's authorship of *Un clerc qui n'a pas trahi* was only definitively established in 1966. See Émile Poulat, "Modernisme et intégrisme: Documents nouveaux," *Revue d'histoire ecclésiastique* 76 (1981): 337–55, at 338–47; "Introduction," *Un clerc qui n'a pas trahi,* 13–18; and *Critique et mystique: Autour de Loisy ou la conscience catholique et l'esprit moderne* (Paris: Le Centurion, 1984): 49–54.

of Loisy and Tyrrell."[4] What, we might therefore ask, did Loisy mean by mysticism when he applied the word to himself? And how might his understanding of mysticism inform our understanding of Modernism?

Loisy did not discuss mysticism at length in anything he published before his excommunication nor, with the exception of a single chapter in the revised edition of *La Religion,* did he develop his ideas for the next two decades. Then, in 1932, Henri Bergson (1859–1941), distinguished philosopher and professor at the Collège de France, published *Les deux sources de la morale et de la religion.*[5] The two sources that Bergson identified were the social instinct and mystical intuition. Loisy, by that time an historian of religions and a colleague of Bergson's at the Collège de France, promptly published a rebuttal entitled *Y-a-t-il deux sources de la religion et de la morale?* in which he set forth his quite different view of mysticism and religion.[6]

Central to Bergson's thesis was the idea that mystics could transcend their historical and social context and then, based on this transcendent experience, introduce a dynamic element into an otherwise static religion. Loisy, on the other hand, was what we would now call a "constructivist." As defined most famously by Stephen Katz, constructivists argue that "the [mystical] experience itself as well as the form in which it is reported is shaped by the concepts which the mystic brings to, and which shape, his experience."[7] For Loisy, constructivism was a claim about history as much as anything else. No human beings, including mystics, could transcend their historical moment and then pull their contemporaries after them. Religious development did not occur

4. Poulat, *Critique et mystique,* 8. Poulat went on to deny the validity of this contrast.

5. Henri Bergson, *The Two Sources of Religion and Morality,* trans. R. Ashley Audra and Cloudesley Brereton, with W. Horsfall Carter (Garden City, N.Y.: Doubleday, 1954). For an accessible overview of Bergson's philosophy as a whole, see Gary Gutting, *French Philosophy in the Twentieth Century* (Cambridge: Cambridge University Press, 2001), 49–83.

6. Alfred Loisy, *Y-a-t-il deux sources de la religion de la morale?* 2nd ed. (Paris, Émile Nourry, 1934). There is no good overview of Loisy's work after 1908, but see the section by Félix Sartiaux in *Alfred Loisy: Sa vie, son oeuvre,* ed. Émile Poulat (Paris: Centre National de la Recherche Scientifique, 1960). For a brief history of how people in France viewed mysticism, see Poulat, *Critique et mystique,* 254–70.

7. Steven T. Katz, "Language, Epistemology, and Mysticism," in *Mysticism and Philosophical Analysis,* ed. Katz (New York: Oxford University Press, 1978), 26.

as a result of the periodic incursion of a dynamic element into otherwise static institutions. Rather it was an ongoing process, all of which stemmed from a basic mystical impulse that Loisy identified as a sense of social solidarity.

The Common Problem

To understand Bergson or Loisy, we must begin at the end. The conclusions of the two books indicate that both Bergson and Loisy considered their debate of vital importance. For the very survival of the species, modern people needed some universal religion that could help human beings live together without killing each other. Writing in the decades after the First World War and just as the Nazi Party was taking power in Germany, both men were acutely aware of the human potential for mutual destruction and the role that religion could play in either increasing or decreasing the danger.

The problem, Bergson argued in his "Final Remarks," was that static societies with their closed moralities had the capacity as well as the instinct to destroy each other. Human beings, he explained, had a natural instinct for war, and natural societies emerged for the purpose of waging war. Unfortunately, people were becoming all too good at fighting. "At the pace at which science is moving," he explained, "that day is not far off when one of the two adversaries . . . will have the means of annihilating his opponent."[8] The question, then, was "to what extent the primitive instinct can be repressed or circumvented?"[9] Bergson was cautiously optimistic, but he concluded, "whether we go bail for small measures or great, a decision is imperative. Mankind lies groaning, half-crushed beneath the weight of its own progress. Men do not sufficiently realize that their future is in their hands. Theirs is the task of determining first of all whether they want to go on living or not. Theirs the responsibility, then, for deciding if they want merely to live, or intend to make just the extra effort required for fulfilling, even on their refractory

8. Bergson, *The Two Sources,* 287.
9. Ibid., 288.

planet, the essential function of the universe, which is a machine for the making of gods."[10]

To decide for life required a cultural transformation, Bergson believed, and mysticism was essential for that transformation. Bergson identified two principal causes of war: overpopulation and overconsumption.[11] After commenting briefly on overpopulation, he emphasized "the concern for comfort and luxury" which had "become the main preoccupation of humanity." Nonetheless, he thought a return to a more "ascetic ideal" possible.[12] "Let a mystic genius but appear," Bergson claimed, and "he will draw after him a humanity already vastly grown in body, and whose soul he has transfigured. . . . Let once the summons of the hero come, we shall not all follow it, but we shall all feel that we ought to, and we shall see the path before us, which will become a highway if we pass along it."[13] While waiting for the mystic genius, he added, science could help by investigating spiritual and psychical phenomena.[14] But by devoting a book to the celebration of the mystical sensibility that transcended the religion and morality of closed societies, he indicated that his ultimate hope lay in the mystical hero.

Loisy diagnosed his contemporary situation similarly. Like Bergson, he identified a "crisis that currently threatened the civilized peoples." Again like Bergson, he believed that this crisis was essentially religious and indeed posed "the problem of a religion of humanity."[15] Too many people, Loisy continued, had parochial loyalties. That loyalty was itself good, he insisted, but it needed expansion. "It is the very sentiment of sociability, of morality, which must be transformed into a complete sense of humanity; it is the power of devotion which is in each for his neighbors, for his fellow citizens, for his country, that must be enlarged by taking for its object the common good . . . of all people."[16]

Where Loisy differed from Bergson was in the way the species might

10. Ibid., 317.

11. Ibid., 289–91.

12. Ibid., 298.

13. Ibid., 311–12.

14. Ibid., 312–17.

15. Loisy, *Y-a-t-il deux sources,* 199–200. Loisy's hope lay in the emergence of a "religion of humanity." On the general idea of a religion of humanity, with reference to Loisy's particular understanding of it, see Poulat, *Critique et mystique,* 230–53.

16. Loisy, *Y-a-t-il deux sources,* 211, cf. 187.

be able to transform each person's natural love of neighbor into a love for all humanity. "The means for realizing [this vision] proposed by Bergson are conceived, in good measure, outside of reality," Loisy insisted.[17] Loisy's own proposal that the League of Nations create an educational agency dedicated to fostering international brotherhood is not any more realistic.[18] What is most relevant for this chapter, however, is less their proposals for achieving world peace and more their competing interpretations of mysticism in the context of the evolution of religion, morality, and society as a whole, and to that we now turn.

Bergson on Mysticism and Religion

Bergson distinguished between morality and religion, and then identified two types of each. He associated mysticism especially with "open morality" and "dynamic religion," although he did not identify mysticism with either so much as argue that it generated both by transforming "closed morality" and "static religion." His definition of mysticism therefore only makes sense in the context of his more general philosophy of morality and religion.

The Two Sources of Morality

Bergson divided his discussion of the two sources of religion and of morality into three sections, the first of which analyzed moral obligation.[19] He approached moral obligation from the standpoint of evolution developed in his earlier work on *L'Evolution créatrice*. In brief, he argued that species had evolved in two opposite directions: into societies governed entirely by instinct, as for example bees or ants; and into societies of individuals with the capacity for exercising independent intelligence, as seen most fully among human beings.[20]

17. Ibid., 200.

18. Ibid., 213.

19. See Dom Illtyd Trethowan, "Bergson and the Zeitgeist—I," *Downside Review* 85 (1967): 138–47, at 138.

20. Bergson, *The Two Sources*, 26–28; Gutting, *French Philosophy*, 66–74, esp. 71–72. Bergson's thought itself clearly evolved over the time separating the two books. On this evolution, see René Violette, *La spiritualité de Bergson* (Toulouse: Éditions Édouard Privat, 1968);

Both types of society survived only by virtue of a sense of social solidarity on the part of their members. "Whether human or animal," Bergson explained, "a society is an organization; it implies a co-ordination and generally also a subordination of elements; it therefore exhibits, whether merely embodied in life or, in addition, specifically formulated, a collection of rules and laws."[21] For bees or ants, this solidarity was instinctive and thus not problematic. Each individual member of the hive naturally subordinated its own interest to the interests of the larger society. For human beings, solidarity was equally important but more problematic. He concluded that rules—a set of moral obligations that people willingly embraced—were a necessary part of any human society.

The basic problem for any human society was therefore ensuring social solidarity by communicating a sense of moral obligation to members who had the capacity to reject the rules of their society. Obligation in the abstract was a natural necessity, but any particular set of obligations was merely conventional.[22] Through the exercise of intelligence, people could reasonably question the obligatory character of the particular rules of their society, thus dangerously undermining social solidarity. Though an evolutionary advantage for the species in many ways, the exercise of intelligence was therefore potentially disruptive as well.

Both morality and religion, at least one sort of morality and one sort of religion, emerged to reinforce the obligatory character of those rules holding society together. Morality, Bergson claimed, began as a set of habits. People developed habits as they were socialized into their community, and this socialization became a kind of second nature that fulfilled the same role that instinct fulfilled for ants.[23] They learned to feel the moral obligations taught them by their society. Religion played the same role, if in a different way. "The first effect of religion," Bergson wrote, "is to sustain and reinforce the claims of society. . . . Religion . . . succeeds in filling the gap, already narrowed by our habitual way of look-

Édouard Rolland, "Le Dieu de Bergson," *Sciences ecclésiastiques* 13 (1961): 83–98, at 84–86. Violette argues that the *Two Sources of Religion and Morality* departs from the philosophy of emanation expressed in *L'Evolution créatrice* and that the consequence is a sometimes odd juxtaposition of claims that do not easily cohere (501, 551–57).

21. Bergson, *The Two Sources,* 27.

22. Ibid., 28–30.

23. Ibid., 9–12.

ing at things, between a command of society and a law of nature."[24] Moral conventions appeared "natural" not only because they were habitual but also because they had a "supernatural" sanction.

When Bergson derived morality from the human need for social cohesion, he explicitly meant the morality associated with what he called "closed societies," societies with strict boundaries between "us" and "them." This association followed from everything he had said about morality to this point. Obligation was natural, but the obligations of any specific society were particular to that society and aimed at preserving its existence. As a consequence, this social morality defined the duties that members of a society had towards each other, not to all human beings. Indeed the social cohesion that gave moral obligation its evolutionary value necessarily excluded outsiders since "social cohesion is largely due to the necessity for a community to protect itself against others."[25]

But the morality of closed societies was not the only form of morality because the evolutionary imperative for social cohesion was not the only source of morality. Bergson identified a second form of morality which he called "human morality," the morality of "an open soul," a soul which did not limit its moral obligations to its immediate community but instead loved all of humanity.[26] Such souls transcended their particular society and, as a consequence, so, too, did their morality. Their morality was not a particular set of rules guaranteeing social cohesion but was rather a response to the life force [*élan vital*] which animated all creation and directed evolution.[27]

Bergson distinguished the two types of morality in a number of ways. For example, the natural morality of the closed society (natural in origin, not in specifics) was imposed on members of a society and took the form of "impersonal habits." By contrast, the human morality was best inculcated through "the imitation of a person, and even a spiritual union, a more or less complete identification."[28] Bergson therefore

24. Ibid., 13.

25. Ibid., 32–33.

26. Ibid., 38.

27. Poulat identifies a series of oppositions that appeared throughout Bergson's book, beginning with closed and open, and ending with nation and humanity (*Critique et mystique*, 271). In this case, we see the connection of open and human in his treatment of morality.

28. Bergson, *The Two Sources*, 35, 39–40, 97.

concluded that though "a substantial half of our morality includes duties whose obligatory character is to be explained fundamentally by the pressure of society on the individual[,] . . . the rest of morality expresses a certain emotional state" that obligates human beings by its drawing power alone.[29] He later referred to these two halves of morality as one of social "pressure" on the individual and one of "aspiration" on the part of the individual towards some higher good.[30]

Bergson acknowledged that the two types of morality tended to blur in human experience.[31] "That which is aspiration," he wrote, "tends to materialize by assuming the form of strict obligation. That which is strict obligation tends to expand and to broaden out by absorbing aspiration . . . . [T]he result is . . . that we lose sight of pure pressure and pure aspiration actually at work on our wills; we see only the concept into which have been melted the two distinct objects to which pressure and aspiration were respectively attached."[32] Furthermore, "pure aspiration is an ideal limit, just like obligation unadorned."[33]

Nonetheless, Bergson insisted on a qualitative difference between social morality and human morality, and he denied that a society could evolve from the former into the latter by a simple process of expansion.[34] "Between a social morality and a human morality," he proclaimed, "the difference is not one of degree but of kind."[35] Hence there were two sources of morality and consequently two types of morality, one associated with closed societies and the other oriented towards the unity of the human race as a whole. The latter, the human morality of aspiration, offered the best hope for the survival and the thriving of the human species in the modern period.

Static Religion

After treating the nature of moral obligation, Bergson turned to religion in his second section. His analysis of religion closely paralleled his

29. Ibid., 49.
30. Ibid., 55. See also Gutting, *French Philosophy,* 75–76.
31. Trethowan, "Bergson and the Zeitgeist—I," 141.
32. Bergson, *The Two Sources,* 65–66.
33. Ibid., 35.
34. Ibid., 38.
35. Ibid., 35.

analysis of morality: here, too, he identified two sources and two types, one closed or "static" and the other open or "dynamic." And again he described the static as the more "natural."[36]

Though religion in general appeared to be a universal human phenomena, Bergson noted that it took many different forms, and he asked to what evolutionary imperative they all responded? Common to all religions was myth, so he narrowed his question: what function did the "myth-making" capacity serve? Immediately he found himself confronted with a paradox. Myth was the product of human intelligence, but particular myths were often absurd and seemed to "thwart our judgment and reason."[37] If human society contrasted with societies of ants because it was based on intelligence rather than instinct, what evolutionary imperative was met by the apparently perverse intellectual act of making myth?

Like social morality, static religion first emerged in response to the need to conserve order by constraining the potentially disruptive exercise of human intelligence, and myth was its primary tool. "[S]ince intelligence works on representations, it will call up 'imaginary' ones, which will hold their own against the representation of reality and will succeed, through the agency of intelligence itself, in counteracting the work of intelligence. This would be the explanation of the myth-making faculty."[38] Myths were "imaginary representations" generated by the intelligence in order to prevent the application of the intelligence from undermining the social order. Bergson concluded that static "religion is then a defensive reaction of nature against the dissolvent power of intelligence."[39] Beneath the tremendous variety of myth and religion across the globe and through human history was a common evolutionary imperative to preserve society against potentially corrosive effects of human intelligence. Myth, and (static) religion more generally, was thus inherently conservative.

But myth was not only conservative; while limiting the free exercise of intelligence in some areas, it could also encourage individuals to take

36. Violette, *La spiritualité de Bergson,* 231–34.

37. Bergson, *The Two Sources,* 109.

38. Ibid., 40.

39. Ibid., 122.

initiative in others. The exercise of intelligence could threaten social stability, but it could also paralyze individuals by making them aware of the inevitability of their own deaths. Myth could help individuals to continue to strive for the good of their society despite the recognition of their mortality by offering some form of hope. To his earlier definition of religion, Bergson therefore added that religion was "a defensive reaction of nature against the representation, by intelligence, of the inevitability of death."[40] Later he expanded this definition to encompass other misfortunes than death: myths were "defensive reactions of nature against the representation, by the intelligence, of a depressing margin of the unexpected between the initiative taken and the effect desired."[41] Religion remained a natural defense against the intelligence, but this time in a way that encouraged productive uses of the intelligence, uses that could help society as a whole to progress. He closed this discussion with the assertion that "belief then means essentially confidence; the original source is not fear, but an assurance against fear."[42]

Bergson went on to analyze in summary fashion a number of issues associated with religion, but his analysis of them need not detain us. More important for our purposes is the functional parallel he saw between religion and morality. Because human societies are governed by intelligence more than by instinct, maintaining social cohesion can be difficult. Nature therefore dictated the need for some form of mutual moral obligation and also some form of myth. Society then dictates the particular moral code and collection of myths that give its members identity and unity over against other social groups. Despite these parallels, however, Bergson explicitly refused to identify religion and morality. History, he insisted, showed that "morality has taken definite shape along its own lines, that religions have evolved along theirs."[43] But one source of each of them was society and particularly the need for social cohesion. And in both cases, this source effectively mandated that they be "closed" and "static."

40. Ibid., 131.
41. Ibid., 140.
42. Ibid., 152.
43. Ibid., 205–6.

Dynamic Religion

However, just as Bergson identified an alternative to closed morality, so he identified an alternative to static religion, and here, at last, we arrive at the heart of the book, Bergson's treatment of mysticism.[44] A particularly strong soul, he said, could "feel itself pervaded, though retaining its own personality, by a being immeasurably mightier than itself.... Its attachment to life would henceforth be its inseparability from this principle.... In addition, it would give itself to society, but to a society comprising all humanity, loved in the love of the principle underlying it. The confidence which static religion brought to man would thus be transfigured."[45] This feeling he called mysticism, and it was the heart of "dynamic religion." Later he defined it as follows: "the ultimate end of mysticism is the establishment of a contact, consequently of a partial coincidence, with the creative effort which life itself manifests. This effort is of God, if it is not God himself. The great mystic is to be conceived as an individual being, capable of transcending the limitations imposed on the species by its material nature, thus continuing and extending the divine action."[46] No longer was the mystic fully subject to the closed morality or static religion of his or her particular society. At least temporarily, he or she experienced some sort of union with God and could relate to all human beings with some approximation of God's love.

Mystical union with God was not complete unless it was manifest in this love for neighbor. Temporary abnormal psychological states like ecstasies or visions often accompanied the experience of mystical union with God, a fact that Bergson argued was "easily comprehensible, if only we stop to think what a shock to the soul is the passing from the static to the dynamic, from the closed to the open, from everyday life to mystic

44. Poulat calls "dynamic" and "mystic" the "governing words of the work" (*Critique et mystique*, 272).

45. Bergson, *The Two Sources*, 212.

46. Bergson always emphasized the importance of intuition. Here he is developing his views on intuition in a specifically mystical direction (220–21). On intuition, see Trethowan, "Bergson and the Zeitgeist—I," 139–40; C. F. Delaney, "Bergson on Science and Philosophy," *Process Studies* 2 (1972): 29–43, at 38–39. On mysticism, see Gutting, *French Philosophy*, 79–80.

life."[47] But ecstasy was only important insofar as it represented this move into union with God; it was not a goal in itself. Rather, Bergson insisted, full union occurred only when the mystic combined action with contemplation, when the mystic experienced union with God while living a life of love in the world.[48] In terms of Bergson's philosophy, the mystic at this point participated in the creative evolution of the human species by allying him or herself with the vital impetus [*élan vital*] which drove human evolution.[49]

Though transcending his or her historical and cultural context, the mystic therefore also necessarily acted within it. Consequently, the mystical impetus did not exist in entire isolation from the religion of the mystic's larger society. "His ecstasies, when they occurred, united him to a God probably greater than anything he had ever conceived, but who did nevertheless correspond to the abstract descriptions with which religion had supplied him."[50] Hence the mystic did not entirely break with the static religion of his or her society. But the point Bergson stressed was that mystical experience could transform an existing religion or initiate a new one. Seen in this light, every new or transformed religion was "the crystallization, brought about by a scientific process of cooling, of what mysticism had poured, while hot, into the soul of man. Through religion all men get a little of what a few privileged souls possessed in full."[51] Mysticism was thus the second source of religion, even for people who might not think of themselves as mystics.

Religion stemmed from both the evolutionary imperative for social solidarity (in so far as it was static) and the mystical intuition of privileged souls (in so far as it was dynamic). Every religion fulfilled the basic evolutionary imperative and therefore was static to some degree, no matter how much inspiration it received from mystics. Bergson could therefore say that "religion is to mysticism what popularization is to science. . . . [M]ysticism is served by religion, against the day when

47. Bergson, *The Two Sources*, 229.

48. Ibid., 231–33; Poulat, *Critique et mystique*, 272. Trethowan discusses the relation of contemplation and action in Bergson's mysticism, and he defends the necessity of contemplation. See "Bergson and the Zeitgeist—II," *Downside Review* 85 (1967): 262–73, at 268–70.

49. Bergson, *The Two Sources*, 234–35.

50. Ibid., 237.

51. Ibid., 238.

religion becomes enriched by . . . mysticism. So then mysticism and religion are mutually cause and effect, and continue to interact on one another indefinitely."[52] On the other hand, some religions had little or no mystical impulse—they were purely static. Speaking about them, Bergson could insist on "a radical difference in nature" between mysticism and religion.[53]

Christianity, Bergson claimed, was, despite its static elements, the greatest example of a dynamic, mystical religion. He acknowledged that it resembled other religions in important respects, deriving many of its particular rites and beliefs from others. But, he insisted, "none of all that was essential; the essence of the new religion was to be the diffusion of mysticism."[54] This mysticism was, of course, grounded in the experience of Christ, who achieved a more perfect union with God than had any other religious teacher,[55] and then it continued, especially among the "great Christian mystics."[56] No other religious tradition could compare. Bergson denied that the Greeks ever achieved pure mysticism[57] or the people of India—Hindus or Buddhists.[58] In so far as modern Hindus like Ramakrishna or Vivekananda reached genuine mystical heights, it was because they had come under the partial influence of Christianity.[59]

How could one best see and discern the relevance of this dynamic religion in action, particularly given that "pure mysticism is a rare essence," and "that it is generally found in a diluted form"?[60] The key was to know what to look for. Historians of religion could most easily trace the outlines and even the development of the static religion that mystics shared with other members of their community.[61] However, Bergson insisted, mysticism gave static religion a new "color and fragrance," resulting in "a mixed religion, implying a new direction given to the old."[62]

52. Ibid., 239.

53. Ibid., 213. On this tension, see Trethowan, "Bergson and the Zeitgeist—II," 266–67.

54. Bergson, *The Two Sources,* 238.

55. Ibid., 239.

56. Ibid., 227; Trethowan, "Bergson and the Zeitgeist—I," 146–47, and "Bergson and the Zeitgeist—II," 262.

57. Bergson, *The Two Sources,* 216–21.

58. Ibid., 221–26.

59. Ibid., 226.

60. Ibid., 213.

61. Ibid., 213, 216.

62. Ibid., 213–14.

If the historian failed to see this dynamic element, "he will have overlooked something, and perhaps the essential."[63] The philosopher could do better so long as he or she began with experience in order to discern "what it has to teach us of a Being Who transcends tangible reality as He transcends human consciousness."[64] Unfortunately, philosophers too often worked in the wrong direction. They first built up an a priori representation and then deduced how life should be from it. Both historians and philosophers should instead begin with an understanding of the nature of dynamic religion and its effect on static religion in order to understand the historical development of religion and its philosophical significance. Most relevantly for our purposes, historians therefore needed a lesson in Bergson's philosophy in order to discern the essence of Christianity and of religion more generally. After reading Loisy's book, he could have offered Loisy as an example of an historian badly in need of such a lesson!

Loisy on Mysticism and Religion

Loisy and Bergson shared much. Both began with a similar assessment of the fundamentally religious character of the crisis that they saw threatening civilization in their day. Both believed that a religious transformation was the best hope for overcoming this crisis. Both worried that religious institutions could discourage progress as easily as encourage it. For Bergson, static religion was the problem. Loisy had finally abandoned Catholicism (and been excommunicated) when he had decided that the Catholic Church could not embrace the modern world and assume leadership of those forces working for progress—in Bergson's terms, he left the Catholic Church because it was static rather than dynamic.

Furthermore, beginning shortly after Loisy's departure from the Church, Bergson and Loisy seem to have recognized each other as fellow travelers. Bergson supported Loisy's election to the Collège de

63. Ibid., 216.
64. Ibid., 262.

France in 1908 and then to the Académie des sciences morales the next year.[65] In notes about his 1908 interview with Bergson written that year, Loisy commented that Bergson "clearly let me understand that, in his view, my teaching, in a neighboring area to his, pursued the same goal as his." Loisy added the comment that "the support of Bergson counted a great deal in my success [in being elected to the Collège], and his benevolence for me has never failed."[66] Loisy also profited from Bergson's ongoing support in his published work. He received Bergson's approval for the draft of his opening lecture to the Collège in May 1909, and, fifteen years later, added a chapter on mysticism to the second edition of *La Religion* in response to Bergson's comments on the first.[67] Loisy commented favorably on Bergson's work in turn, particularly on *L'Evolution créatrice,* offering it as an example of philosophy that was not driven by ideology or dogma but was rather "scientific." He even acknowledged his "affinities with the school of 'intuition,' if by that one meant the philosophy of Bergson."[68] Coming from Loisy, such an acknowledgement is striking. The overall picture that emerges from a survey of references to Bergson in Loisy's *Mémoires* is not one of close friends, but Bergson and Loisy seem to have read each other's work with general approval, and Loisy praised Bergson in print at least as late as 1931 (the year he released the third volume of his *Mémoires*). And yet Loisy devoted a book to refuting Bergson's philosophy of religion shortly thereafter. What was so significantly wrong about Bergson's proposals? Quite a lot, it turns out.[69]

65. Loisy, *Mémoires,* 3:69, 82–83. See also Normand Provencher, "Les letters de Henri Bergson à Alfred Loisy," *Église et Théologie* 20 (1989): 425–38, at 425–26; Poulat, *Critique et mystique,* 254–59.

66. Loisy, *Mémoires,* 3:69.

67. Ibid., 3:104, 348. Loisy first published *La Religion* in 1917 and issued the revised second edition in 1924. In a number of letters to Loisy, Bergson thanked him for the gift of some recent books and commented favorably upon it. For Bergson's comments on the first edition of *La Religion,* see Bergson to Loisy, 20 July 1917, in Provencher, "Lettres," 427–28.

68. Loisy, *Mémoires,* 3:366–67, 381.

69. See Poulat, *Critique et mystique,* 276–77. Poulat acknowledges weaknesses in Loisy's book, but claims that the issues raised in his debate with Bergson merit serious attention nonetheless.

History versus Philosophy

Loisy's objections stemmed in part from his methodological differences from Bergson. For decades, going back into his Modernist period, Loisy had insisted historical scholarship be free of theological or philosophical presuppositions and instead rely on those facts that historians could ascertain based on the available evidence. Philosophy and theology followed from history, in his view, not the reverse. One of the virtues of Bergson's earlier philosophical work had been precisely its reliance on science rather than ideology, but here Bergson had reversed the direction. When he spoke of the "causes" of religion and morality, he "did not mean only their immediate and historical sources, those which are observable in living people and the documents of the human past. He meant as well and above all the metaphysical principle of *élan vital*." Bergson then used this principle "to explain the data of history and psychology."[70] Going back as far as his Modernist writings from the turn of the century, Loisy had always insisted on doing the opposite: using history to assess philosophy. In the first sentence of his preface, he denied that he had any inclination for "questions of a purely speculative order,"[71] and in the first chapter he promised to "examine from a purely historical and psychological viewpoint" the claims Bergson made about religion and morality.[72] Not surprisingly, he found that Bergson's claims failed to account adequately for the data of history, and, Loisy concluded, his basic philosophy of religion and morality was therefore incorrect. But Loisy's first objection was that Bergson approached history from a philosophical and metaphysical perspective rather than approaching philosophy from a properly historical one.[73]

Given his methodological differences from Bergson, Loisy naturally differed from him on many particular historical claims, especially about early Christianity, to which we will return below. However (ironically!) we must begin by examining Loisy's philosophy of history and the way it differed from Bergson's.

70. Loisy, *Y-a-t-il deux sources,* 19.

71. Ibid., i.

72. Ibid., 19–20, cf. 11.

73. See, for example, Loisy, *Y-a-t-il deux sources,* 34. See also Poulat, *Critique et mystique,* 278.

Like Loisy, Bergson was interested in the historical process by which societies evolved. He saw this evolution as a natural ebb and flow as action called forth opposing reaction, and he tried to articulate general laws governing this process of historical development.[74] However this process was not necessarily a smooth one, as his discussion of static and dynamic religions indicated. Static religions did not naturally develop into dynamic ones. Left alone, they simply stayed the same, continuously discouraging any exercise of the intelligence that might disrupt social solidarity. Into this closed system came a mystical intuition of God, which propelled the religion in a more open direction until it could resume stasis in some transformed shape. Nature could not account for this mystical impulse, so, Loisy deduced, Bergson considered it to be "supernatural in the strongest sense of the word."[75] Evolution, then, occurred not simply as an organic process from within the society but rather as an incursion from outside it. In Loisy's words, Bergson alleged "a clear break in the evolution because the notion of a good God, a God of love, and the notion of universal humanity do not come naturally from national religions."[76]

Loisy disputed this model of historical development on two grounds. First, he rejected Bergson's search for a transcendent, supernatural source of evolutionary power in favor of the natural, historical development of society itself. Second, he denied the discontinuity that Bergson saw in history as a result of these divine incursions. Loisy acknowledged the fact of change, of course, but insisted that it occurred as a part of the natural life of any religion without the sharp breaks that Bergson wanted to identify. For example, he surveyed the development of different views of sacrifice as well as the development from magical incantations to prayer.[77] In neither case did he find dramatic transformations. Speak-

74. Loisy, *Y-a-t-il deux sources,* 292–98.

75. Ibid., 14. See also Violette, *La spiritualité de Bergson,* 253. Ironically, some Catholic writers criticized Bergson for inadequately distinguishing between nature and the supernatural, between creation and creator. See, for example, Rolland, "Le dieu de Bergson," 86–93; R. Jolivet, "Philosophie chrétienne et Bergsonisme," *Revue des sciences religieuses* 15 (1935): 28–43, at 34–40.

76. Loisy, *Y-a-t-il deux sources,* 150.

77. For his comments on sacrifice, Loisy could draw on his *Essai historique sur le sacrifice*

ing specifically of prayer, he concluded that it had been "spiritualized and moralized more and more without denying its point of departure or changing its orientation" in magic.[78] And the continuities he found in religious practice did "not happen without a certain continuity of spirit."[79] Against Bergson, Loisy defended a developmental view of history that did not proceed by sudden incursions of God so much as by natural and cultural processes that historians could trace. This was the orthodoxy of the historian, as Loisy understood history, and Bergson's theory had inappropriately challenged it.[80]

Instead of identifying two broad types of religion that interacted within history but that had fundamentally different sources, Loisy saw a continuous process of religious evolution. He distinguished three types of religion: primitive, national, and universal. The religions of primitive people offered material blessings in this life; the national religions of more civilized peoples stressed the well-being of the nation; and the universal religions offered personal immortality or eternal salvation. But, he immediately added, his categories were not mutually exclusive. Primitive religion included some sense of the well-being of the larger society and some sense of individual immortality, at least in germinal form. The universal religions did not entirely abandon the promise of material prosperity or national well-being. Loisy thus emphasized the historical continuity between the different types of religion; one type could evolve into another type (and presumably back again). Translated into Bergson's terms, Loisy argued, "from the standpoint of the historian, the religion called dynamic issued from static religions; it developed from them naturally and progressively, not by an abrupt leap and by the sudden explosion of a religion transcending all that had preceded it."[81]

(Paris: Émile Nourry, 1920), which he had sent to Bergson. See Bergson to Loisy, 28 June 1920, in Provencher, "Lettres," 429.

78. Loisy, *Y-a-t-il deux sources,* 85.

79. Ibid., 92.

80. Loisy had taken essentially this position as early as 1898, when he published (as A. Firmin) "Le développement chrétien d'après le cardinal Newman," *Revue du clergé français* 17 (1898): 5–20. For a contemporary response explicitly written from the perspective of the history of religions, see A. Vincent, "Les religions statiques et dynamiques de M. Bergson et l'histoire des religions," *Revue des sciences religieuses* 15 (1935): 44–58, at 56–58. A Catholic, Vincent rejected Loisy's view that all religious history was continuous in this way.

81. Loisy, *Y-a-t-il deux sources,* 55.

Static and *Dynamic*

Given his emphasis on historical continuity, Loisy rejected the distinctions of moral and religious types so fundamental to Bergson's argument. Though Bergson acknowledged that the morality of pressure and static religion on the one hand, and the morality of aspiration and dynamic religion on the other had been mixed in historical experience, he still insisted that they were "essentially different," Loisy noted. The former stemmed from natural society and the latter from heroic individuals.[82] However, Loisy asked rhetorically, were not "dynamism and conservation two aspects of [religious] evolution from its beginning?"[83] Historians, he insisted in answer to his own question, could easily determine that neither "immobile, purely static" religions nor purely dynamic ones had ever existed.[84] He added that "one discerns less easily the conformity of [Bergson's distinctions] with the human realities which are here to be interpreted."[85]

Bergson's false dichotomy between static and dynamic religions derived from another false dichotomy that he drew: that between individuals and society. For Bergson, the needs of society determined the features of closed morality and static religion, while the aspirations and intuitions of privileged individuals were "open" and "dynamic." In both cases, Loisy believed, the contrast was too great. We have already seen Loisy's rejection of Bergson's claim that mystics could transcend their cultural and historical context. Loisy refused to accept this picture of individuals operating outside of society, a point that had been central to his much earlier polemic against liberal Protestantism.[86] Religion, even the religion of the mystic, was necessarily social.

Loisy was just as unsympathetic to Bergson's claims about the pressures society exerted on the individual, however. If Bergson's treatment of dynamic religion was consistent with his philosophy of élan vital, his

82. Ibid., 20–21.

83. Ibid., vii.

84. Ibid, 7, 13, 25, and 129.

85. Ibid., 22. See also Vincent, "Les religions statiques et dynamiques," 47–50. On this point, Vincent agreed with Loisy against Bergson.

86. See, especially, A. Firmin [Loisy], "La théorie individualiste de la religion," *Revue du clergé français* 17 (1899): 202–15.

analysis of closed societies drew on Durkheim's sociology, Loisy insisted, and he had long disputed Durkheim's tendency to reify society.[87] Many years before, he had ended an extensive review of Durkheim's *Les formes élémentaires de la vie religieuse* by praising Durkheim's emphasis on the role of society in religion, but also taking him to task. Durkheim, Loisy had argued, "has not constructed a science of religion and of society; he has constructed a metaphysic of the one and the other. He works in absolute logic while claiming to explain a reality that is perpetually changing." As we have seen, Loisy said the same about Bergson. Then, Loisy concluded, "is it necessary to abstract society from the individuals who compose it?"[88] He repeated this point against Bergson here: "the two sources [of religion and morality] . . . presented as disparate [that is, society and the individual] are joined in reality. . . . [I]n the order of existence and of human history, societies consist only of individuals."[89] To speak of the conservative force of society on individuals as if society had an existence separate from the individuals comprising it struck Loisy as misleading. And if the historian of religions could not speak of the individual and society as separate entities, each capable of producing its own type of religion, then there were not two types of religion deriving from them.

The Nature of Christianity

The single most important religious tradition for both Bergson and Loisy was, of course, Christianity, and their different claims about it clearly reflected their larger philosophical differences. According to Bergson, Jesus introduced a dynamic element into the static religion of his day and an open, universal love ethic into an essentially closed morality. As a consequence, he marked a dramatic break with first century Judaism and its historical antecedents, and Bergson celebrated the transformation that he wrought.[90] Jesus' relationship to the prophets

87. Loisy, *Y-a-t-il deux sources,* iv.

88. Loisy, "Sociologie et religion," *Revue d'histoire et de literature religieuses,* n.s. 1 (1913): 75–76.

89. Loisy, *Y-a-t-il deux sources,* 22–23.

90. Trethowan, "Bergson and the Zeitgeist—I," 144–45. Violette argues that Bergson's

best exemplified both his originality and the way that he nonetheless drew from the religious tradition that he inherited. Bergson explicitly hesitated "to classify the Jewish prophets among the mystics of antiquity." Still, he added, Jesus could "be considered as the continuator of the prophets of Israel," and Bergson acknowledged the contribution of the prophets to the distinctively "active mysticism" characteristic of Christianity.[91] In this case, we can see how mystical experience transcended a particular cultural and historical context in order to introduce something new, but also how it interacted with and drew on that same context. Dynamic religion (Jesus) fundamentally differed from static religion (first-century Judaism), but then merged with it in a new, transformed synthesis (Christianity).

Bergson did not develop these claims about Jesus at great length, but he had strayed into an area of particular strength for Loisy, and Loisy attacked him on historical grounds. Bergson had explicitly sidestepped some of the difficult questions about the historical Jesus and the witness of the gospels because his primary claim about Jesus was precisely that he had escaped history through his mystical union with God. What mattered about Jesus, according to Bergson as Loisy understood him, was his paradigmatic and "intuitive perception of the God of love that the great mystics have had in ecstatic experiences."[92] But this was not what the gospels actually said. "[T]he synoptic tradition does not show Jesus as an ecstatic" in Bergson's sense, he claimed, and even the gospel of John portrayed Jesus differently in some important respects.[93] Bergson had simply imposed his philosophy on them. Further, Loisy accused Bergson of Marcionism for essentially repudiating the religion of Israel in the name of a pure religion taught by Jesus, despite his best efforts to "nuance as much as he could the relationship of

recognition of this break and subsequent transformation effected a radical change in Bergson's thinking, moving him from a philosophy of emanation to a personalism that was far more compatible with orthodox Christianity (*La spiritualité de Bergson,* 492–96). Violette goes on to say that Bergson saw more continuity between "living Judaism" and Catholicism in his final years (514–15).

91. Bergson, *The Two Sources,* 240.

92. Loisy, *Y-a-t-il deux sources,* 32, cf. 36.

93. *Ibid.,* 43–45. See also Poulat, *Critique et mystique,* 281–83.

Christianity with Judaism."[94] Loisy unfairly implied that ecstasy was a necessary part of mysticism in Bergson's view, and in accusing Bergson of Marcionism, he clearly exaggerated Bergson's rejection of the religion of Israel. But insofar as Bergson insisted that Jesus' religion was genuinely mystical and thoroughly original, and that it thus transcended his religious context, Loisy seems appropriately to have applied Bergson's general claims to the case of Christianity, Bergson's nuances notwithstanding.

If Bergson's treatment of Jesus reflected his philosophical understanding of the interplay between dynamic and static religions, Loisy's quite different approach to understanding Jesus reflected his competing assumption that historical development was a continuous process without dramatic interruptions. Noting that the root of Christianity was Jewish, Loisy tried to understand Jesus *within* his religious context rather than over against it.[95] And looked at in context, Jesus appeared to share with other Jews the apocalyptic hope of the imminent arrival of the kingdom of God. This idea, rather than Bergson's mysticism of divine love, dominated Jesus' preaching, as Loisy had argued for three decades, going back to *L'Évangile et l'Église,* his attack on the liberal Protestantism of Adolf von Harnack.[96] Thus understood, Jesus was part

94. Loisy, *Y-a-t-il deux sources,* 56. In the same year that he published *Y-a-t-il deux sources de la religion et de la morale?* Loisy also released a revised and expanded edition of *La religion d' Israel,* 3rd ed. (Paris: Émile Nourry, 1933) and *La naissance du christianisme* (Paris: Émile Nourry, 1933), both of which he sent to Bergson.

95. Loisy, *Y-a-t-il deux sources,* 62.

96. Ibid., 63, 145–46. A great deal has been published on Loisy's exchange with Harnack. See, for example, Bernard Brandon Scott, "Adolf von Harnack and Alfred Loisy: A Debate on the Historical Methodology of Christian Origins"(Ph.D. diss, Vanderbilt University, 1971), 211–306, and his "Introduction" to the English translation of *The Gospel and the Church,* trans. Christopher Home (Philadelphia: Fortress Press, 1976), xliii–lxiv; Stephen Sykes, *The Identity of Christianity* (London: SPCK, 1984), 123–46; Émile Poulat, *Histoire, dogme et critique dans la crise moderniste* (Tournai: Casterman, 1962), 46–73, 89–102; Dietmar Bader, *Der Weg Loisys zur Erforschung der Christlichen Wahrheit* (Freiburg: Herder, 1974), 65–172; Marcel Simon, "À propos de la crise moderniste: Écriture et tradition chez Alfred Loisy," in *Text, Wort, Glaube: Studien zur Überlieferung, Interpretation und Autorisierung biblischer Texte,* ed. M. Brecht (Berlin: de Gruyter, 1980), 360–64; Diether Hoffmann-Axthelm, "Loisys L'Évangile et l'Église: Besichtigung eines zeitgenössischen Schlachtfeldes," *Zeitschrift für Theologie und Kirche* 65 (1968): 296–309; Harvey Hill, "La science catholique: Alfred Loisy's Program of Historical Theology," *Zeitschrift für neuere Theologiegeschichte/Journal for the History of Modern Theology* 3 (1996):

of an ongoing process of historical development rather than a dramatic break within history.

Bergson's interpretation of subsequent Christian history fared no better. Few Christians, Loisy asserted, could have recognized Bergson's mysticism as their own faith. The mysticism that Bergson emphasized as central to the Christian tradition applied only to Pseudo-Dionysius and various figures during the Middle Ages and the Reformation. It "appertains to the history of the Church," he acknowledged, but it did not define the whole.[97] Furthermore, even those Christians whose experiences did resemble Bergson's description of pure mysticism differed in some significant ways from each other.[98] Loisy seems to have meant that scholars should not speak of a transcendent experience shared by different mystics even within the same tradition or historical period. In other words, he radically rejected Bergson's assertion that mystics transcended their religious and historical context. The mystics themselves did not claim such transcendence, Loisy added. Christian mystics claimed to be Christians in the normal sense of that term, not singular, dynamic figures in an otherwise static religious institution.[99] Even the great Christian mystics were thus more or less normal Christians participating in the ongoing process of historical development in a more or less normal way.

For Loisy, then, the historian could appropriately study high Christian mysticism as part of the religious evolution of Christianity, not the whole of it, and Christianity was itself part of the ongoing religious evolution of the species, not its terminal point. "The great Christian mystics had precursors in all the religions. And who would dare to say now that they did not receive in their inheritance any of the imperfections inherent to the religions of the centuries of ignorance?"[100] Again, "[t]o see in high Christian mysticism the perfect religion that nothing had prepared, that nothing must follow," he wrote, "is to divide arbitrarily the

39–59, and *The Politics of Modernism: Alfred Loisy and the Scientific Study of Religion* (Washington, D.C.: The Catholic University of America Press, 2002), 117–32.

97. Loisy, *Y-a-t-il deux sources,* 64.

98. Ibid., 147.

99. Ibid., 61, 147–48. See also Violette, *La spiritualité de Bergson,* 253–54.

100. Loisy, *Y-a-t-il deux sources,* 152–53.

history of religions and the history of Christianity. This history is still in progress . . . Christian mysticism marks a stage of religious evolution; it is not the absolute crown of religious evolution."[101] In other words, Loisy insisted on continuity between Christianity and other religions, particularly Judaism, and within Christianity he saw genuine development even among the mystics. The mysticism within Christianity was not all the same, and it did not differ in absolute ways from other forms of religious experience, Christian or not. There was no divine incursion from outside of history, and there was no dramatic break within human history, even in Christianity.

For Loisy, many of these issues were familiar from old fights. In broad terms, Bergson's philosophy resembled the historical theology of Adolf von Harnack to which Loisy had responded in his most famous Modernist work, *L'Évangile et l'Église*. Like Bergson, Harnack had identified a pure form of religion that he associated with Jesus. Like Bergson, Harnack had acknowledged that Jesus' pure religion was necessarily expressed in particular historical forms even if it transcended any particular historical context. Like Bergson, Harnack emphasized a feeling of union with and love for God, which was then expressed in love for other people. Without mentioning Harnack by name, Loisy linked Bergson and his liberal Protestant predecessor. "That the Christ of the gospel was the first to feel and to reveal the God of love, several notable representatives of liberal Protestantism had said before Bergson," he noted.[102] And as he had replied to Harnack, so Loisy replied to Bergson that his effort to limit mysticism to some "pure" form associated with Jesus and existing largely unchanged despite changing historical con-

101. Ibid., 65.

102. Ibid., 62. Loisy also said that although Catholic apologists liked Bergson's book, they would have condemned him as a Modernist had he been Catholic (173). Camille de Belloy surveys selected Catholic responses in "Bergsonisme et Christianisme: Les Deux Sources de la Morale et de la Religion au Jugement des Catholiques," *Revue des sciences philosophiques et théologiques* 85 (2001): 641–67. Several Catholic philosophers have written on the relation of Bergson's philosophy and Christianity. See, for example, H. Gouhier, *Bergson et le Christ des évangiles* (Paris: Fayard, 1962); Violette, *La spiritualité de Bergson*; Rolland, "Le dieu de Bergson"; Jolivet, "Philosophie chrétienne et Bergsonisme"; and B. Montagnes, "La philosophie et le Christianisme," *Revue des sciences philosophiques et théologiques* 47 (1963): 407–19, at 407–11.

texts was historically untenable.[103] The "superior essence" of Christianity which Bergson claimed to have discovered "has never been realized in the history of Christian societies as an existing religion. It is useless to add that Christian morality has undergone the same vicissitudes as religion."[104] Loisy himself had changed in many ways since his 1902 polemic with Harnack, but he was consistent in his attempts to explain Christianity historically in terms of gradual historical development, not as some pure and essential experience that transcended history.

Mysticism as the Single Cause of Religion and Morality

Having rejected Bergson's analysis of religion and morality, Loisy offered his own alternative account of the "origin, character, and future of religion and morality."[105] First, Loisy attacked Bergson's distinction between religion and morality. Primitive societies did not distinguish between religion and morality, he insisted, but rather linked the two, and "the initial relationship between morality and religion has never been broken in the course of history in the closed societies which have succeeded each other on our globe."[106] In Loisy's own day, philosophers had tried to construct theories of morality independent of religion, and these efforts had even taken concrete form when the Third Republic had tried to secularize moral education in the public schools around the turn of the century. But despite these efforts, "the secularization of morality even among our contemporaries scarcely exists except in theory."[107] Looking forward, Loisy noted that Bergson himself envisioned an ultimate conjunction of perfect religion and perfect morality. Loisy agreed, and commented that "it is doubtless that morality and religion have never been absolutely separable nor entirely separated."[108] When Loisy offered his own explanation of the causes of religion and morality, he therefore treated religion and morality together.

What, then, was the origin of religion and morality, according to

103. Loisy, *Y-a-t-il deux sources,* 36.

104. Ibid., 193.

105. Ibid., vii.

106. Ibid., 121.

107. Ibid., 122. On Loisy's early response to the effort to secularize moral education, see Harvey Hill, "Loisy's 'Mystical Faith': Loisy, Leo, and Sabatier on Moral Education and the Church," *Theological Studies,* 65 (2004): 73–94.

108. Loisy, *Y-a-t-il deux sources,* 128.

Loisy? At first glance, Loisy did not disagree with Bergson about the origin of religion very dramatically. Like Bergson, Loisy believed that both morality and religion arose as a product of an original sense of social solidarity. For Loisy, however, this sense of social solidarity was itself mystical, not the antithesis of mysticism. Based on the etymology of the word mysticism, Loisy linked it to religious initiation in the Hellenistic world. Originally, the term meant initiation into a secret society that somehow guaranteed blessed immortality.[109] Mysticism in this sense was a feature of universal religions, but Loisy traced the basic practice back to initiation in primitive societies, the ritual introducing young men "into the social life of the tribe by an intervention of the spirit who is believed to be, in one manner or another, the creator and guardian of it."[110] As in this example, so more generally, religious rituals produced and reinforced the mystical character of social solidarity, and the sense of moral obligation stemmed from it.[111] Thus understood, the basic mystical act was to join the individual to a larger society, and the emotional experience that accompanied the act was identical with the feeling of social solidarity that Bergson had identified as the source of static religions and social morality.

Given this identification of mysticism and social solidarity, Loisy refused to postulate a religion of the individual mystic alongside the religion of society. Indeed, speaking of an individual mystic separate from his or her social context made no sense since the basic mystical experience was itself an experience of social solidarity. Loisy concluded that "mysticism, religion, and the spirit of human sociability are originally and by nature one and the same thing."[112] This was not a new idea for him. At least as early as 1924, he said the same in a chapter added to *La Religion* at Bergson's suggestion. Indeed, he had used precisely the same words to make his point.[113] His book-length refutation of Bergson was thus the development of ideas he had been considering for a decade.

All religion as well as all morality stemmed from this primitive sense of social solidarity without regard to Bergson's distinctions of

109. Ibid., 33.
110. Ibid., 35.
111. Ibid., 116–17.
112. Ibid., 35.
113. Loisy, *La Religion,* 2nd ed. (Paris: Émile Nourry, 1924), 14.

static and dynamic, closed and open. Loisy first defended the mystical character of the so-called static religions. "The sentiment of the unity of a clan, of a tribe, is," he said, "already a very real sentiment, a mystical sentiment of humanity perpetually living. The entire future of the idea of humanity was in that humble beginning because it was the intimate and profound sense of solidarity . . . an essentially moral idea, religious idea, mystical idea."[114] He made the same point in his final summary of "The Origin of Religion and Morality" (ch. 1). "At the beginning in primitive societies there was only a single source of morality and religion . . . : the religious sentiment, which is the first source of morality and of religion. . . . To this single source is attached the moralities of closed societies and the static religions of the same societies."[115] Loisy called this religious sentiment mysticism and discussed primitive religions, particularly totemism, and the "national religions," including the religion of Israel, concluding that mysticism was at the root of both.[116]

Second, Loisy argued, against Bergson, that dynamic religions evolved naturally from static ones. After noting that the sense of solidarity was the source of religion and morality in closed societies, he quickly added, "We do not hesitate to see there the immediate source of open morality and of the religion of pure love."[117] Bergson assumed that the sense of social solidarity led to closed societies because people were naturally hostile to outsiders. Loisy disputed the point: members of one society were not inevitably hostile to members of another.[118] People learned to value their union with other members of their own society as they developed a sense of mystical solidarity with them. Nothing more than inherited prejudice prevented these same people from expanding their sense of who was included in their society. Loisy therefore preached a natural development towards greater openness without appealing to some supernatural cause as the agent of this development, Bergson notwithstanding.[119] Loisy summarized his point as follows: "a single morality [and, he might have added, a single religious impulse] has ruled on earth since the beginning, the morality of

114. Loisy, *Y-a-t-il deux sources,* 153.
115. Ibid., 29–30.
116. Ibid., 48–58.
117. Ibid., 29–30, cf. v–vi.
118. Ibid., 107, 111.
119. Ibid., 109, 107.

solidarity, but it needs to progressively enlarge its perspectives in order to realize itself in its fullness."[120]

When Loisy identified mysticism as the sense of social solidarity in this way and claimed that it was the single source of all religions and all forms of morality, he dramatically broadened the meaning of the term "mystic." Instead of identifying a mystical type of religion and a parallel but distinct mystical type of morality, which appealed to certain people with mystical sensibilities, as Bergson had done, Loisy claimed that all religions, all moralities, and all people were mystical. Strictly speaking, he could not discuss mysticism alongside religion as if some form of religion were not mystical. Rather, mysticism was "coextensive with . . . religion, a certain mysticism existing . . . in all the religions."[121] The same was true of individuals. Rhetorically he asked "if it is not true that humanity, in all of its representatives, is naturally mystical to different degrees."[122] This was an important point of contention between the two. Was mysticism the province of a small elite, or were all people mystics to some degree? Bergson took the former position, and Loisy took the latter.[123]

Of course, Loisy was not a perennialist, arguing that all religions were ultimately the same. If "the impulses of mysticism are produced in all times, in all human milieux," he also insisted that they were produced "in different senses, with different degrees of success, and these impulses do not lead very simply in a single direction."[124] All stemmed from a sense of social solidarity, the same sense of social solidarity that made human society possible, but particular societies took different forms and could be more or less inclusive. Loisy was well aware of the ways in which religion could serve as a tool of domination promoting xenophobia, and also of the consequent need for people of good will to work towards a "religion of humanity" based on a mystical solidarity linking all people.[125] This work, he argued, need not wait on some mystical genius, but was rather the basic human task.

120. Ibid., 115.

121. Ibid., 32.

122. Ibid., vi.

123. Bergson highlighted this difference in a letter a letter to Loisy dated 16 December 1936, in Provencher, "Les letters," 433–34. See also Poulat, *Critique et mystique,* 280–81.

124. Loisy, *Y-a-t-il deux sources,* 149.

125. Ibid., 208–13.

Conclusion

If we follow the titles of the two works under consideration, we can summarize the basic argument as follows. Bergson identified two sources of religion and morality: the evolutionary imperative of social solidarity generated static religion and closed morality, while mystical intuition introduced more dynamic and open features. As a source of religion, mysticism drove the process of historical development forward despite the conservative force of static religion. In reply, Loisy asked if there were indeed two sources of religion and morality, and he answered in the negative. The social solidarity that Bergson linked to static religion and closed morality was in fact the single source of all religion and all morality. Bergson misrepresented this sense of social solidarity, denying its genuinely mystical character and wrongly suggesting that the religion that stemmed from it was static. In fact, the dynamic religion that Bergson associated with mysticism was really just a feature of static religion, and the pure, transcendent mysticism that he distinguished from social solidarity did not exist. Mysticism was not a break in the natural, social, or historical order, but was rather itself natural, social, and historical.

So who wins the argument? Inevitably, the question is too complicated to resolve simply. Loisy was the superior historian. His account of the religion of Israel, the historical Jesus, and the development of the Christian spiritual tradition corrected some of Bergson's claims and revealed the degree to which Bergson did indeed import his own philosophy into his historical sources, as Loisy claimed. Although contemporary scholars working on the historical Jesus might not agree with Loisy's particular historical claims about him, virtually all of them interpret Jesus in terms of his historical context much more than did Bergson. Whatever else he was, Jesus was a first-century Jew more than a Bergsonian mystic.

On the other hand, Loisy loses points because he overstated his differences with Bergson. Despite Loisy's claims to the contrary, Bergson recognized that his ideal types did not exist in history. Mystics did not, and could not, transcend their social contexts so entirely as to mark a total break with the religion they inherited. Even Jesus, religious innovator though Bergson claimed him to be, drew on the legacy of the prophets who preceded him. And if Christianity was the only religion to achieve a pure mysticism, other religions did at least experience some mystical impulses. In so far as Loisy failed to acknowledge these nuances, he refuted an oversimplified version of Bergson's philosophy, not Bergson's more subtle philosophy itself. In a letter to Loisy, Bergson said as much: "there is almost no passage cited [from my book in yours]," he wrote, "which does not refer, as a commentary often counter to yours, to other passages in the *Deux Sources*."[126] In fact, Bergson's distinctions of dynamic and static seem helpful in identifying different impulses that appear within religions, just not as a classification system for different religions themselves. Bergson himself could well have accepted this qualification.

Their different views of mysticism are more difficult to assess. Bergson claimed to identify some pure mystical experience that transcended any single cultural context, even if expressed within it. This claim can seem naïve in the academy today when contrasted to Loisy's counterclaim that mystics remained embedded in their historical and social contexts. Most scholars of religion today seem to share Loisy's constructivism. And if no one had a more or less pure mystical experience along the lines suggested by Bergson, his entire system collapses. On the other hand, Loisy's identification of mysticism with the sense of social solidarity seems reductionistic. It corresponded to his interpretation of religious history and established a firm theoretical foundation for the religion of humanity that he hoped to see develop. But it did not correspond to the descriptions that many mystics have given of their experiences. For example, the mystical theology of Pseudo-Dionysius does not seem to be based on a sense of social solidarity. But without some such reductionistic definition of mysticism, the word could easily become so broad as to be meaningless for Loisy. After all, if every religion and every person is mystical, to call something mystical means nothing.

126. Bergson to Loisy, 12 November 1933, in Provencher, "Lettres," 434–35. On Bergson's reactions, see Poulat, *Critique et mystique*, 259.

Perhaps the problem is with the category of the mystical itself. Although we can make fruitful comparisons between particular mystics within and across traditions, defining mysticism in the abstract with sufficient precision to be meaningful and with sufficient breadth to include those people generally regarded as mystics seems to be impossible. Bergson tried to be scientific in his definition of mysticism and to reflect on its philosophical implications, but he ultimately limited pure mysticism to Jesus. Loisy was more historically sensitive, but he, too, ended in speculation about the origin and nature of religious experience, and his speculations could well be challenged by many religious people. As much as anything else, then, the debate between Bergson and Loisy illustrates the difficult of speaking meaningfully about a category of experience that is on the one hand so common and on the other so difficult to conceptualize.

Bibliography

Adams, J. L. "Letter from Friedrich von Hügel to William James." *Downside Review* 98 (1980): 214–36.

Archidec, Alain. *Ferdinand Brunetière ou la rage de croire.* 2 vols. Diss., L'Université d'Aix-en-Provence, 1974.

Bader, Dietmar. *Der Weg Loisys zur Erforschung der Christlichen Wahrheit.* Freiburg: Herder, 1974.

Barmann, Lawrence. *Baron Friedrich von Hügel and the Modernist Crisis in England.* Cambridge: Cambridge University Press, 1972.

———. "Friedrich von Hügel as Modernist and as More Than Modernist." *Catholic Historical Review* 75 (1989): 211–32.

———. "Baron Friedrich von Hügel and Mysticism: In Pursuit of the Christian Ideal." In *Sanctity and Secularity During the Modernist Period,* edited by Lawrence Barmann and C. J. T. Talar. Brussels: Société des Bollandistes, 1999.

———. "The Modernist as Mystic." In *Catholicism Contending with Modernity: Roman Catholic Modernism and Anti-Modernism in Historical Context,* edited by Darrell Jodock. Cambridge: Cambridge University Press, 2000.

Baruzi, Jean. *Saint Jean de la Croix et le problème de l'expérience mystique.* Paris: Éditions Salvador, 1999.

Bergamo, Milo. *La Science des saints.* Grenoble: Jérôme Millon, 1992.

Bergson, Henri. *The Two Sources of Religion and Morality.* Translated by R. Ashley Audra and Cloudesley Brereton, with W. Horsfall Carter. Garden City, N.Y.: Doubleday, 1954.

Bernard-Maitre, Henri. "A propos de 'L'Histoire littéraire du Sentiment religieux': Une correspondence de Bremond avec Loisy (1924–1929)." *Revue d'ascétique et mystique* 45 (1969): 161–89.

Bertoldi, Francesco. "Il dibattio sulla verità tra Blondel e Garrigou-Lagrange." *Sapienza* 43 (1990): 293–310.

Blanchet, André. *Histoire d'un mise à l'Index: la "Sainte Chantal" de l'Abbé Henri Bremond*. Paris: Aubier Montaigne, 1967.

———. *Henri Bremond 1865–1904*. Paris: Aubier-Montaigne, 1975.

———, ed. *Henri Bremond–Maurice Blondel. Correspondance,* 3 vols. Paris: Aubier Montaigne, 1970–1971.

Blondel, Maurice. "L'illusion idéaliste." *Revue de Métaphysique et de Morale* 6 (1898): 726–45.

———. "Le point de départ de la récherche philosophique." *Annales de philosophie chrétienne* 151 (1906): 337–60; 152 (1906): 225–50. Translated by Fiacre Long as "The Starting Point of Philosophical Research." In *The Idealist Illusion and Other Essays.* Dordrecht: Kluwer Academic, 2000.

———. "Le procès de l'intelligence." In *Le procès de l'intelligence,* edited by Paul Archambault. Paris: Bloud et Gay, 1922.

———. "Le problème de la mystique." In *Qu'est-ce que la mystique? Cahiers de la nouvelle Journée*. Paris: Bloud et Gay, 1925: 1–63.

———. *L'Action I–II*. Presses Universitaires de France, 1947.

———. *L'Action (1893): Essai d'un critique de la vie et d'une science de la pratique*. Paris: Presses Universitaires de France, 1950. Translated by Oliva Blanchette as *Action (1893): Essay on a Critique of Life and a Science of Practice.* Notre Dame: University of Notre Dame Press, 1984.

———. *La Pensée II: Les Responsibilités de la Pensée et la Possibilité de son Achèvement*. Paris: Presses Universitaires de France, 1954.

———. *Carnets intimes (1882–1894)*. Paris: Éditions du Cerf, 1961.

Bouillard, Henri. *Blondel and Christianity*. Translated by James Somerville. Washington: Corpus Books, 1969.

Bourdieu, Pierre. *Science of Science and Reflexivity*. Chicago: University of Chicago Press, 2004.

Bourgeois, Henri. "Passivité et activité dans le discourse et l'expérience de madame Guyon." In *Madame Guyon*. Grenoble: Jérôme Millon, 1977.

Boutié, L. "Fénelon: D'après quelques critiques contemporains." *Études* 66 (1895): 542–69.

———. *Fénelon*. Paris: Victor Retaux, 1899.

Bremond, Henri. *Newman I. Le développement du dogme Chrétien*. Paris: Librairie Bloud, 1905, 2nd ed., 1906.

———. *Newman II. Psychologie de la foi*. Paris: Librairie Bloud, 1905.

———. *Newman III. La vie Chrétienne*. Paris: Librairie Bloud, 1906.

———. *Newman. Essai de biographie psychologique*. Paris: Bloud & Gay, 1906. Translated by H. C. Corrance as *The Mystery of Newman.* London: Williams & Norgate, 1907.

———. "Pro Fenelone." *Annales de philosophie chrétienne* 9 (1909–1910): 223–44; 337–71; 472–518; 10 (1910): 20–53.

———. "Fénelon et la critique psychologique." *Annales de philosophie chrétienne* 9 (1909–1910): 144–62.

———. *Apologie pour Fénelon.* Paris: Perrin, 1910.

———. "Une crise dans la vie intérieure de Bossuet." *Annales de philosophie chrétienne* 15 (October 1912–March 1913): 258–71.

———. *Histoire littéraire du sentiment religieux en France, depuis la fin des guerres de religion jusqu'à nos jours,* 11 vols. [1915–1933]. Republished in 5 vols. Grenoble: Jérôme Millon, 2006.

———. *Bossuet, maître d'oraison.* Paris: Bloud & Gay, 1931.

———. *La querelle du Pur Amour au temps de Louis XIII.* Paris: Bloud et Gay, 1932.

Briggs, Charles L., ed. *Disorderly Discourse: Narrative, Conflict, and Inequality.* Oxford: Oxford University Press, 1996.

Bronfen, Elisabeth. *The Knotted Subject: Hysteria and Its Discontents.* Princeton: Princeton University Press, 1998.

Brunetière, Ferdinand. "La querelle du quiétisme." [1881] *Études critiques sur l'histoire de littérature française* 2. Paris: Librairie Hachette, 1922.

———. "Fénelon." [1893] *Études critiques sur l'histoire de littérature française* 2. Paris: Librairie Hachette, 1922.

Bruyère, Cécile. *The Spiritual Life and Prayer.* [1900] Eugene, Or.: Wipf and Stock, 2002.

Burke, Ronald. "Loisy's Faith: Landshift in Catholic Thought." *Journal of Religion* 60 (1980): 138–64.

Cagnac, Moïse. *Fénelon: Études critiques.* Paris: Société française d'imprimiere et de librairie, 1910.

Charcot, J.-M. "La foi qui guérit." *La Revue hebdomadaire* 7 (December 1892): 112–32.

Cherel. Albert. *Fénelon ou la religion du pur amour.* Paris: Denoël et Steele, 1934.

Clark, John. *La Pensée de Ferdinand Brunetière.* Paris: Librairie Nizet, 1954.

Cognet, Louis. *Post-Reformation Spirituality.* Translated by P. Hepburne Scott. New York: Hawthorne Books, 1959.

———. *La crépuscule des mystiques.* Paris: Desclée, 1995.

Colin, Pierre. *L'audace et le soupcon: La crise moderniste dans le catholicisme français (1893–1914).* Paris: Desclée de Brouwer, 1997.

Combe, Pierre. *Histoire de la restauration du chant grégorien d'après des documents inédits.* Sablé sur Sarthe: Abbaye de Solesmes, 1969. Translated by Theodore N. Marier and William Skinner as *Restoration of Gregorian Chant: Solesmes and the Vatican Edition* (Washington, D.C.: The Catholic University of America Press, 2003).

Crouslé, L. *Fénelon et Bossuet, études morales et littéraires,* 2 vols. Paris: Honoré Champion, 1894.

de Belloy, Camille. "Bergsonisme et Christianisme: Les Deux Sources de la Morale et de la Religion au Jugement des Catholiques." *Revue des sciences philosophiques et théologiques* 85 (2001): 641–67.

de Boyer de Saint-Suzanne, Raymond. "Alfred Loisy et la religion du pur amour." *Commentaire* 3 (1978): 304–15.

de Caussade, Jean-Pierre. *On Prayer: Spiritual Instructions on the Various States of Prayer According to the Doctrine of Bossuet, Bishop of Meaux.* Translated by Algar Thorold. Springfield, Ill.: Templegate, 1960.

de Certeau, Michel. *The Mystic Fable.* Vol. 1, *The Sixteenth and Seventeenth Centuries.* Translated by Michael B. Smith. Chicago: University of Chicago Press, 1992.

de la Bedoyère, Michael. *The Archbishop and the Lady.* New York: Pantheon, 1956.

de Lubac, Henri. *Augustinianism and Modern Theology.* Translated by Lancelot Sheppard. New York: Herder and Herder, 1969.

Davis, Natalie Zemon. "The Quest of Michel de Certeau." *New York Review of Books* 55 (May 15, 2008).

Delacroix, Henri. *Études d'histoire et de psychologie du mysticisme.* Paris: Félix Alcan, 1908.

———. "Remarques sur 'Une grande mystique.'" *Journal de psychologie normale et pathologique* (July 15, 1925): 545–84.

Delaney, C. F. "Bergson on Science and Philosophy." *Process Studies* 2 (1972): 29–43.

[Delatte, Paul]. *Dom Guéranger. Abbé de Solesmes,* 2 vols. Paris: Plon-Nourrit, 1909–1910.

Delfour, Abbé. Le procès de Fénelon." *Revue du clergé français* 5 (1895): 214–28.

Diefendorf, Barbara B. *From Penitence to Charity: Pious Women and the Catholic Reformation in Paris.* Oxford: Oxford University Press, 2004.

Dru, Alexander, and Illtyd Trethowan. *Maurice Blondel: The Letter on Apologetics and History and Dogma.* [1964] Grand Rapids, Mich.: Eerdmans, 1994.

Dupré, Louis. "Mysticism." In *The Encyclopedia of Religion,* edited by Mircea Eliade. New York: Macmillan, 1987.

———. *The Enlightenment and the Intellectual Foundations of Modern Culture.* New Haven: Yale University Press, 2004.

Firmin, A. [Alfred Loisy]. "Le développement chrétien d'après le cardinal Newman." *Revue du clergé français* 17 (1898): 5–20.

———. "La théorie individualiste de la religion." *Revue du clergé français* 17 (1899): 202–15.

Fouilloux, Étienne. *Une Église en quête de liberté. La penseé catholique entre modernisme et Vatican II, 1914–1962.* Paris: Desclée de Brouwer, 1998.

Franklin, R. W. *Nineteenth-Century Churches: The History of a New Catholicism in Wüttemberg, England, and France*. New York: Garland Publishing, 1987.

Goichot, Émile. "En marge de la crise moderniste: La correspondance Bremond-von Hügel." *Revue des sciences religieuses* 48 (1974): 209–34; 49 (1975): 202–33; 53 (1979): 124–46.

———. "Une très haute, très séduisante, une fatale figure. Bremond et Madame Guyon." *Madame Guyon*. Grenoble: Jérôme Millon, 1977.

———. *Henri Bremond, Historien de sentiment religieux*. Paris: Éditions Ophrys, 1982.

———. *Alfred Loisy et ses amis*. Paris: Cerf, 2002.

Goré, Jeanne-Lydie. *La notion de l'indifférence chez Fénelon au sujet du quiétisme du Madame Guyon*. Paris: Presses Universitaires de France, 1956.

———. *L'itinéraire de Fénelon: Humanisme et spiritualité*. Paris: Presses Universitaires de France, 1957.

Gouhier, Henri. *Bergson et le Christ des évangiles*. Paris: Fayard, 1962.

———. *Fénelon philosophe*. Paris: J. Vrin, 1977.

Guépin, Alphonse. *Solesmes et Dom Guéranger*. Le Mans: Edmond Monnoyer, 1876.

Guéranger, Prosper. *Histoire de sainte Cécile*. Tournai: J. Casterman, 1851. Translated as *Life of Saint Cecilia*. Philadelphia: Peter F. Cunningham, 1866.

Guinan, Alastair. "Portrait of a Devout Humanist: M. l'Abbé Bremond." *Harvard Theological Review* 47 (1954): 15–53.

Gutting, Gary. *French Philosophy in the Twentieth Century*. Cambridge: Cambridge University Press, 2001.

Harent, Stéphane. "A propos de Fénelon: La question de l'amour pur." *Études* 127 (1911): 178–96, 349–63, 480–500, 745–68.

Heidegger, Martin. "The Question Concerning Technology." In *Basic Writings*, edited by David Farrell Krell. San Francisco: HarperSan Francisco, 1993.

Henrici, Peter. *Hegel und Blondel*. Pullach: Verlag Berchmanskolleg, 1958.

Hill, Harvey. "La science catholique: Alfred Loisy's Program of Historical Theology." *Zeitschrift für neuere Theologiegeschichte/Journal for the History of Modern Theology* 3 (1996): 39–59.

———. "More Than a Biblical Critic: Alfred Loisy's Modernism in Light of His Autobiographies." In *Personal Faith and Institutional Commitments: Roman Catholic Modernist and Anti-Modernist Autobiography,* edited by Lawrence Barmann and Harvey Hill. Scranton, Penn.: University of Scranton Press, 2002.

———. *The Politics of Modernism: Alfred Loisy and the Scientific Study of Religion*. Washington, D.C.: The Catholic University of America Press, 2002.

———. "Loisy's 'Mystical Faith': Loisy, Leo, and Sabatier on Moral Education and the Church." *Theological Studies* 65 (2004): 73–94.

Hillenar, Henk. "Madame Guyon et Fénelon." *Madame Guyon*. Grenoble: Jérôme Millon, 1977.

Hoffmann-Axthelm, Diether. "Loisys L'Évangile et l'Église: Besichtigung eines zeitgenössichen Schlachtfeldes." *Zeitschrift für Theologie und Kirche* 65 (1968): 296–309.

Hogarth, Henry. *Henri Bremond: The Life and Work of a Devout Humanist.* London: SPCK, 1950.

Houtin, Albert. *Dom Couturier, Abbé de Solesmes*. Angers: Germain & G. Grassin, 1899.

———. "Notes sur les profès de l'abbaye de Solesmes." *La Province du Maine* XIX (1911): 167–73, 191–98, 229–38, 271–77, 292–95, 327–33, 361–67, 385–91.

———. *Histoire du modernisme catholique.* Paris: Chez l'auteur, 1913.

———. *Une grande mystique. Madame Bruyère.* Paris: Alcan, 1925, 2nd ed., 1930.

———. *Une vie de prêtre*. Paris: Rieder, 1926. Translated by Winifred S. Whale as *The Life of a Priest.* London: Watts & Co., 1927.

———. *Ma vie laïque*. Paris: Rieder, 1928.

In spiritu et veritate. Solesmes: Sainte-Cécile de Solesmes, 1966.

James, William. *The Varieties of Religious Experience.* [1902] New York: New American Library, 1958.

Jantzen, Grace M. *Power, Gender and Christian Mysticism*. Cambridge: Cambridge University Press, 1995.

Johnson, Cuthbert. *Prosper Guéranger (1805–1875): A Liturgical Theologian.* Rome: Pontificio S. Anselmo, 1984.

Jolivet, R. "Philosophie chrétienne et Bergsonisme." *Revue des sciences religieuses* 15 (1935): 28–43.

Joppin, Gabriel. *Fénelon et la mystique du pur amour*. Paris: Gabriel Beauchesne, 1938.

Katz, Steven T. "Language, Epistemology, and Mysticism." In *Mysticism and Philosophical Analysis,* edited by Steven T. Katz. New York: Oxford University Press, 1978.

Kelly, James. "The Abbé Huvelin's Counsels to Baron Friedrich von Hügel." *Bijdragen Tijdschrift voor Filosofie en Theologie* 39 (1978): 59–69.

Kerlin, Michael J. "Blondel and Pragmatism: Truth as the Real Adequation of Mind and Life." In *The Reception of Pragmatism in France and the Rise of Roman Catholic Modernism, 1890–1914,* edited by David Schultenover. Washington, D.C.: The Catholic University of America Press, 2009.

Knowles, David. "What Is Mysticism?" In *Understanding Mysticism,* edited by Richard Woods. Garden City, N.Y.: Image Books, 1980.

Krumenacker, Yves. *L'école française de spiritualité*. Paris: Cerf, 1998.

Lalande, André. *Vocabulaire technique et critique de la philosophie*. Paris: Librairie Félix Alcan, 1926.

Lash, Nicholas. "Modernism, Aggiornamento and the Night Battle." In *Bishops and Writers, Aspects of the Evolution of Modern English Catholicism,* edited by Adrian Hastings. Wheathampstead: Anthony Clarke, 1977.

Laver, James. *The First Decadent*. New York: Citadel Press, 1955.

Le Brun, Jacques. *La spiritualité de Bossuet*. Paris: Librairie C. Klincksieck, 1972.

Ledru, Ambroise. *Dom Guéranger, Abbé de Solesmes et Mgr Bouvier, Évêque du Mans*. Paris: Honoré Champion, 1911.

Le Roy, Edouard. *Dogme et critique*. Paris: Bloud, 1907.

Libouroux, Ch. *Controverse entre Bossuet et Fénelon au sujet du quiétisme de Madame Guyon*. Paris: Victor Palmé, 1876.

Loisy, Alfred. *L'Évangile et l'Église*. Paris: Alphonse Picard, 1902. Translated by Christopher Home as *The Gospel and the Church*. [1903] (Philadelphia: Fortress Press, 1976).

———. *Choses passées*. Paris: Émile Nourry, 1913. Translated by Richard W. Boynton as *My Duel with the Vatican* [1924]. New York: Greenwood Press, 1968.

———. "Sociologie et religion." *Revue d'hsitoire et de littérature religieuses,* n.s. 1 (1913): 45–76.

———. *La religion*. Paris: Émile Nourry, 1917, 2nd ed. 1924.

———. *Essai historique sur le sacrifice*. Paris: Émile Nourry, 1920.

———. *Mémoires pour servir à l'histoire religieuse de notre temps,* 3 vols. Paris: Émile Nourry, 1930–1931.

———. *La naissance du christianisme*. Paris: Émile Nourry, 1933.

———. *La religion d'Israel*. 3rd ed. Paris: Émile Nourry, 1933.

———. *Y-a-t-il deux sources de la religion et de la morale?* 2nd ed. Paris: Émile Nourry, 1934.

———. *George Tyrrell et Henri Bremond*. Paris: Émile Nourry, 1936.

Loome, Thomas. "The Enigma of Baron Friedrich von Hügel." *Downside Review* 91 (1973): 13–34, 123–40, 204–30.

Louis-David, Ann. *Lettres de George Tyrrell à Henri Bremond*. Paris: Aubier Montaigne, 1971.

McKeown, Elizabeth. "After the Fall: Roman Catholic Modernism at the American Academy of Religion." *U. S. Catholic Historian* 20 (2002): 111–13.

Marlé, René. *Au coeur de la crsie moderniste*. Paris: Aubier Montaigne, 1960.

Mazzoni, Christina. *Saint Hysteria: Neurosis, Mysticism, and Gender in European Religious Culture*. Ithaca: Cornell University Press, 1996.

Montagnes, Bernard. "La philosophie et le Christianisme." *Revue des sciences philosophiques et théologiques* 47 (1963): 407–19.

Murata, Mayumi. "Les reactions de Fénelon d'après la condemnation." In *Fénelon. Mystique et politique (1699–1999)*, edited by F. X. Cuche and J. Le Brun. Paris: Honoré Champion, 2004.

O'Connell, Marvin. *Critics on Trial: An Introduction to the Catholic Modernist Crisis*. Washington, D.C.: The Catholic University of America Press, 1994.

Olphe-Galliard, Michel. *La théologie mystique en France au XVIIIe siècle. Le Père de Caussade*. Paris: Beauchesne, 1984.

Oury, Guy-Marie. *Dom Guéranger. Moine au Coeur de l'Église*. Solesmes: Éditions de Solesmes, 2000.

———. *Lumière et force: Mère Cécile Bruyère, première abbesse de Sainte Cécile. Solesmes*: Éditions de Solesmes, 2005.

Pacheu, Jules. *L'Expérience mystique et l'activité subconsciente*. Paris: Perrin, 1911.

Petre, Maude. *Von Hügel and Tyrrell: The Story of a Friendship*. London: Dent, 1937.

———. *Alfred Loisy. His Religious Significance*. Cambridge: Cambridge University Press, 1944.

———. "Quiétisme." In *Dictionnaire de spiritualité*. Vol. 12, col. 2756–842.

Portier, Lucienne. *Un précurseur: L'abbé Huvelin*. Paris: Cerf, 1979.

Poulain, Augustin. *Des Grâces d'oraison*. Paris: Gabriel Beauchesne, 1931. Translated by Leonora L. Yorke Smith as *The Graces of Interior Prayer* (St. Louis: B. Herder, 1951).

Poulat, Émile, ed. *Alfred Loisy, sa vie, son oeuvre*. Paris: Centre National de la Recherche Scientifique, 1960.

———, ed. *Une oeuvre clandestine d'Henri Bremond: Sylvain LeBlanc, Un Clerc qui n'a pas trahi: Alfred Loisy d'après ses Mémoires*. Rome: Edizioni di Storia e Letteratura, 1972.

———. "Modernisme et intégrisme: Documents nouveaux." *Revue d'histoire ecclésiastique* 76 (1981): 337–55.

———. *Critique et mystique: Autour de Loisy ou la conscience catholique et l'esprit moderne*. Paris: Le Centurion, 1984.

———. *Histoire, dogme et critique dans la crise moderniste*. Tournai: Casterman, 1962.

———. *L'Université devant la mystique*. Paris: Éditions Salvador, 1999.

Provencher, Normand. "Les lettres de Henri Bergson à Alfred Loisy." *Église et théologie* 20 (1989): 425–38.

Récéjac, E. *Essai sur les fondaments de la connaissance mystique*. Paris: Félix Alcan, 1897. Translated by Sara Carr Upton as *Essay on the Bases of Mystic Knowledge*. New York: Scribner's, 1899.

Rolland, Édouard. "Le Dieu de Bergson." *Sciences ecclésiastiques* 13 (1961): 83–98.

Rousseau, Olivier. *The Progress of the Liturgy*. Westminster, Md.: The Newman Press, 1951.

Sanks, T. Howland. *Authority in the Church: A Study in Changing Paradigms*. Missoula, Mont.: Scholars Press, 1974.

Saudreau, Auguste. *L'État mystique*. Paris: Vic & Amat, 1903. Translated as *Mystical State: Its Nature and Phases*. London: Burns Oates & Washbourne, 1924.

———. *Les Faits extraordinaires de la Vie spirituelle*. Paris: Vic & Amat, 1908.

Schmidt, Leigh Eric. "The Making of Modern Mysticism." *Journal of the American Academy of Religion* 71 (2003): 273–302.

Schwalm, M.-Bénoit. "Les illusions de l'idéalisme et leurs dangers pour la foi." *Revue Thomiste* 4 (1896): 413–41.

Scott, Bernard Brandon. "Adolf von Harnack and Alfred Loisy: A Debate on the Historical Methodology of Christian Origins." PhD diss., Vanderbilt University, 1971.

Showalter, Elaine. "Hysteria, Feminism and Gender." In *Hysteria beyond Freud*, Sander L. Gilman, et al. Berkeley: University of California Press, 1993.

Simon, Marcel. "À propos de la crise moderniste: Écriture et tradition chez Alfred Loisy." In *Text, Wort, Glaube: Studien zur Überlieferung, Interpretation und Authorisierung biblischer Texte*, edited by M. Brecht. Berlin: de Gruyter, 1980.

Soltner, Louis. *Solesmes and Dom Guéranger 1805–1895*. Translated by Joseph O'Connor. Brewster, Mass.: Paraclete Press, 1995.

Sykes, Stephen. *The Identity of Christianity*. London: SPCK, 1984.

Taves, Ann. *Fits, Trances, & Visions*. Princeton: Princeton University Press, 1999.

Trethowan, Illtyd. "Bergson and the Zeitgeist." *Downside Review* 85 (1967): 138–47, 262–73.

Varillon, François. *Fénelon et le pur amour*. Paris: Éditions du Seuil, 1957.

Vidler, Alec. *A Variety of Catholic Modernists*. Cambridge: Cambridge University Press, 1970.

Vincent, A. "Les religions statiques et dynamiques de M. Bergson et l'histoire des religions." *Revue des sciences religieuses* 15 (1935): 44–58.

Violette, René. *La spiritualité de Bergson*. Toulouse: Éditions Édouard Privat, 1968.

Von Hügel, Friedrich. "The Church and the Bible: Two Stages in Their Inter-Relation." *The Dublin Review* 231 (1894): 313–41; 233 (1895): 306–37; 235 (1895): 273–304.

———. *The Mystical Element of Religion as Studied in Saint Catherine of Genoa and Her Friends*, 2 vols. London: Dent, 1908, 2nd ed. 1923.

———. *Essays and Addresses on the Philosophy of Religion*. 1st series. London: Dent, 1921.

———. "Louis Duchesne." *The Times Literary Supplement* 1062 (May 25, 1922).

———. *Essays and Addresses on the Philosophy of Religion*. 2nd series. London: Dent, 1926.

Ward, Wilfrid. *William George Ward and the Catholic Revival*. London: Macmillan, 1893.

Worgul, George. "Maurice Blondel and the Problem of Mysticism." *Ephemerides theologiae Lovanienses* 61 (1985): 100–22.

Contributors

LAWRENCE BARMANN is professor emeritus at Saint Louis University. He was a longtime member of the Roman Catholic Modernism Working Group/Seminar of the American Academy of Religion. He has written extensively on Baron Friedrich von Hügel, including *Baron Friedrich von Hügel and the Modernist Crisis in England* (1972).

HARVEY HILL is associate professor of religion at Berry College. His primary areas of interest include Roman Catholic Modernism, historical consciousness, and religion and nature. His books include *The Politics of Modernism: Alfred Loisy and the Scientific Study of Religion* (2002) and, with Louis-Pierre Sardella and C. J. T. Talar, *By Those Who Knew Them: French Modernists Left, Right, and Center* (2008), both published by the Catholic University of America Press.

MICHAEL J. KERLIN was professor of philosophy at LaSalle University for forty-two years and chairman of the department from 1972 to 2000. He was a member of the Roman Catholic Modernism Working Group/Seminar of the American Academy of Religion for over thirty years. He published numerous articles on philosophy of religion, philosophy of history, and business and society issues. His essay "Blondel and Pragmatism: Truth as the Real Adequation of Mind and Life" can be found in David G. Schultenover, ed., *The Reception of Pragmatism in France and the Rise of Roman Catholic Modernism, 1890–1914* (The Catholic University of America Press, 2009).

In his final hospitalization for leukemia, Michael kept the conversation going on the topics that had consumed his life—philosophy, religion, and the broader world. He died on November 23, 2007, having completed his last article, "Maurice Blondel: Philosophy, Prayer, and the Mystical."

WILLIAM L. PORTIER holds the Mary Ann Spearin Chair of Catholic Theology at the University of Dayton. A historical theologian, he works in nineteenth- and twentieth-century U.S. Catholicism. His books include *Isaac Hecker and the First Vatican Council* (1985) and *Divided Friends: Portraits of the Roman Catholic Modernist Crisis in the United States* (forthcoming).

C. J. T. TALAR is professor of systematic theology at the University of Saint Thomas. He was co-convener of the Roman Catholic Modernism Seminar (1995–1999) and has worked on John Henry Newman and modern French Catholicism. He is coauthor, with Harvey Hill and Louise-Pierre Sardella, of *By Those Who Knew Them: French Modernists Left, Right, and Center* (2008), and his chapter on Marcel Hébert appears in David G. Schultenover, ed., *The Reception of Pragmatism in France and the Rise of Roman Catholic Modernism, 1890–1914* (2009), both published by the Catholic University of America Press.

Index

Modernists and Mystics was designed and typeset in Arno by Kachergis Book Design of Pittsboro, North Carolina. It was printed on 60-pound House Natural Smooth and bound by Sheridan Books of Ann Arbor, Michigan.